EXTRAORDINARY
DOGS

Joyce Darrell; Foreword by Warren Eckstein

Inspirational Stories of Dogs with Disabilities

EXTRAORDINARY

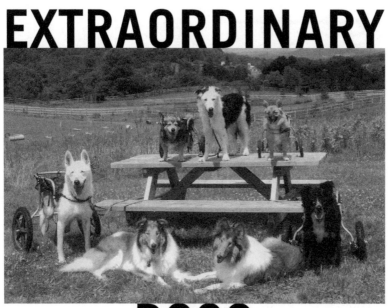

DOGS

THE LYONS PRESS
Guilford, Connecticut
An imprint of The Globe Pequot Press

The Lyons Press is an imprint of The Globe Pequot Press.

10 9 8 7 6 5 4 3 2 1

Printed in the United States of America
Designed by Diane Gleba Hall
Cover photograph by Betsy Testerman

Library of Congress Cataloging-in-Publication Data

Darrell, Joyce, 1962–
     Extraordinary dogs : inspirational stories of dogs with disabilities / Joyce Darrell.
       p.   cm.
ISBN 978-1-59921-049-0
       1. Dogs with disabilities.   I. Title.
SF992.D46D37 2007
636.7—dc22
                              2006101490

Extraordinary Dogs is dedicated to the memory of
Pauline Chaney and Ed Farrell,
two people who have changed our lives forever.
We miss you both and think about you every day.

*   *   *

. . . and to one great dog named Princess.
Not a day goes by that we don't credit Princess
for rescuing Duke from our local shelter.

Inseparable pals: Princess and Duke,
before his accident.

Joyce Darrell, her husband, Michael, and the rest of their family.

Contents

Foreword

Courage and Devotion on Four Legs

Since this world is so full of sadness and negativity, meeting Duke and Misty was like a breath of fresh air. I would like to share my story of Duke and Misty—two mischievous mutts with huge hearts—with you.

I met these spirited and lively pets and their caretakers, Joyce and Mike, while I was doing a segment on the *Today* show about unusual pet products. The focus of my segment was showing wheelchairs for dogs, and I wanted dogs that had been actually using them to appear with me on air. What I expected was a couple of nice, mellow dogs that were able to use the wheelchair, but when Duke and Misty arrived at the studio in New York City, I was amazed to find two feisty dogs that had no idea they had any type of disability. They were running, jumping, playing ball, and basically getting into as much trouble as any other dog would, maybe even a little more. But what stood out the most for me was the admiration these two dogs had for Mike and Joyce, and vice versa.

When people ask if these dogs would be better off being "put to sleep," the only answer I can come up with is to tell them to just watch the determination in these dogs' eyes and their will to live life to the fullest—and to look at the genuine smiles on the faces of Mike and Joyce.

As we go though life, we have the opportunity to meet some special people. Mike and Joyce are two examples of *very* special people who have brought tons of awareness to the public about adopting dogs (and other animals as well) with special needs. And one could not ask for better dogs to support this cause than Duke and Misty.

As you read *Extraordinary Dogs*, you will meet more exceptional people with inspirational tales of how they came together with their loving canine companions. It takes a lot of patience and understanding to take care of dogs with special needs—be it because of paralysis, blindness, deafness, or missing limbs—but the lifetime friendships formed will be a great reward.

All these dogs, and their caretakers, are heroes in my eyes.

Warren Eckstein
Pet Behaviorist and
Nationally Syndicated
Radio Show Host

Acknowledgments

M ike and I are so appreciative to Kaleena Cote and The Lyons Press for making this book a reality and giving much needed exposure to pets with disabilities. Thank you for bringing Pets with Disabilities, our nonprofit organization dedicated to helping and promoting the adoption of physically disabled animals, into mainstream America.

We are also thankful to the following people: our Web master John Rycyna, who has spent so many countless hours working on the Pets with Disabilities Web site, a great tool that has been crucial in getting dogs with special needs adopted; Jill Barsky, a believer in our mission, and our voice when we really need one; Dewey Springer, founder of Dewey's Wheelchairs for Dogs, for making great wheelchairs and always being there for us when we need another one; Betsy Testerman, who continues to donate so much of her time by helping our organization in more ways than she knows; and Lillie Goodrich and John Andersen, great friends we made through rescue efforts and founders of Glen Highland Farm, who provide wonderful trail walks that are welcoming to all of our dogs with disabilities. A big thank you to Nick and Charlene Scala, a young couple who opened up their hearts and home to a great dog named Hoops who needed a special home.

Thanks to all the "Extraordinary People" who have adopted dogs with disabilities, and who have contributed their stories to this book.

And last but not least, a big thank-you to Virginia and Bill Johnson, along with their three blind collies, Lady, Emma, and Sadar who have been with us from the very beginning in helping us spread the word on how these amazing dogs with disabilities can—and will—touch your heart.

Introduction

We clearly remember the day that Duke broke his back. Faced with so many decisions, many people kept telling us we should just take the easy way out and euthanize him. "What kind of life will he have?" numerous vets hypothetically asked us. To be honest, we weren't sure.

But if you could have only *seen* the look in Duke's eyes that day—almost as if saying, *Please, just give me a chance*—there was no way a person with any sort of compassion could simply put this dog to sleep. Then and there my husband, Mike, and I made a decision that would ultimately change our lives forever.

* * *

A few months after Duke's injury, another smaller disabled dog came into our lives. Misty, a feisty corgi mix, had been sitting in a New York animal shelter for over five years. No one wanted her because she needed a wheelchair to get around. She was considered a throwaway dog to everyone who passed her by—that is, until Mike and I caught wind of her. We didn't think twice as we got into our car and drove to the shelter to adopt her. We were eager to let her start living the life she fully deserved to live.

When Duke was injured, we thought there had to be some sort of support group out there that offered information on how to care for pets with disabilities—or at least where we could go and talk with other people who owned disabled dogs. I mean, there are support groups for everything, right? Apparently we were wrong. After looking through phone books and surfing the Internet, we couldn't find anything. We realized why Misty had been on her own for so long—no one knew how to care for her properly. We also realized we were on our own.

There was a definite need for such a group and so we decided to take matters into our hands. We also figured we would need spokesdogs for the cause—and already we had the perfect candidates. This gave birth to Pets with Disabilities, a grassroots organization with a few human volunteers and some great dogs (Duke and Misty) to help other dogs in need and to show animal owners that living with a pet with a disability is definitely, well, not far-fetched.

Today, we travel all over the United States with our dogs promoting awareness. Over the years, Pets with Disabilities has been instrumental in helping shelters, humane societies, and breeders find good homes for their dogs with special needs. We have managed to give a voice and a face (in the form of an energetic, fun-loving, sloppy-kissing German shepherd mix and his little partner in crime) and, more important, hope for dogs with disabilities.

The Pets with Disabilities organization is not only about finding homes for dogs and other animals with disabilities, it's about changing people's misconceived perceptions of these lovable creatures. As you read each story in *Extraordinary Dogs*,

Duke doing one of his favorite activities.

you'll realize how unique each dog really is and how much personality each one actually has. However, all the characteristics I'm
sure you'll grow to love come out partly because of the very special
bonds every dog has with its caretaker. We are their bridge to the
able-bodied world. Whether it is the comfort of hearing, seeing,
or having wheels placed on them, they know who cares for them
and they appreciate it.

Please, as you turn each page and gaze upon each tail-wagging
pup, do not feel sorry for any of them. You'd be quite surprised

at what these dogs are capable of. They're just so happy to be running, jumping, playing—to be alive. These dogs are the best pets we will ever encounter. What they don't know is that while we help make their lives a little easier, they do the exact same for us. Thank you for taking the time to read *Extraordinary Dogs* and we hope you walk away with a better understanding of these wonderful beings.

Joyce Darrell, Cofounder
Pets with Disabilities

Duke

*Joyce Darrell, Small Business Owner and Cofounder of
Pets with Disabilities; Mike Dickerson, Elevator Mechanic
and Cofounder of Pets with Disabilities*

My husband, Mike, and I decided that we wanted to expand our "family" and adopt another dog to keep our older dog company. Traveling to our local shelter to check out what was available, we didn't have any expectations. As soon as we got there, though, immediately one particular high-energy pup grabbed our attention—barking like crazy, wagging his tail a mile a minute, and jumping around in his cage as if to say, "Hey, you! Over here! Pick me! Pick me!" All we had to do was look at him and it was a done deal. A week later Duke became one of our own. Little did we know our lives were about to be changed forever.

You wake up each morning wondering what life has in store for you that day. For most people, the daily grind continues on as usual but sometimes, for unknown reasons, yours gets shaken up a bit.

Mike and I were visiting our friend, Ed, who had just adopted two puppies of his own. Often, I would bring Duke over to play with Ed's menagerie of mutts in his huge fenced-in yard. His home was a safe haven for dogs—no one ever had to worry about cars or

I

trucks speeding by. It was amusing to watch these wild and reckless puppies frolicking and somersaulting all over each other, that is, until Duke let out a sudden yelp.

We ran over to see what was wrong, but Duke stood motionless. Scooping him up, we rushed to the veterinarian's office, thinking he was going to be OK. We were wrong. The X-rays revealed that Duke had broken his spinal cord. Oddly enough, despite the trauma, he was still able to wag his tail and look at us with the same hopeful eyes that initially won us over. We knew we had a special pet on our hands. The vet explained our options—we could go forward with risky surgery to repair Duke's spine or we could euthanize him—but the second choice was out of the question.

Optimistic, the surgeon told us that Duke had a good chance of being able to walk again. However, the procedure didn't go as

well as planned and we ended up receiving a phone call later that night from the vet suggesting that we put him down. We refused, and the vet continued to try and fix our tough little puppy—but it wasn't enough.

Four days later, Duke was paralyzed. Without a plan or knowledge on how to care for a paralyzed pet, we took it one day at a time. My husband would sleep with Duke on our kitchen floor to keep the dog stabilized. We even worked his lifeless legs in a kiddy pool, hoping he would regain some movement. But, as the weeks went by, we realized Duke had suffered permanent spinal damage. Something different had to be done.

We weren't sure how Duke would react to using a customized wheelchair, but as soon as it arrived and we strapped him in, we knew we made the right choice. Duke would zip around everywhere in his new wheelchair—his lifeline—and he soon became stronger and more confident than ever.

Because of his ordeal and its outcome, he has become a spokesdog for his cause and for our grassroots organization, Pets with Disabilities—educating people all over the country about pet paralysis and helping rescue groups place animals with disabilities in caring homes. Not a day goes by that he doesn't continue to amaze people with his overall zest for life. He truly is an inspiration on wheels.

Duke's needs are basic—he likes a good scratching, fresh food, and a warm home, just like any other dog. Although his care demands a bit more from us than his four-legged friends, it has all definitely been worthwhile. We have gone from not knowing how to support our disabled dog to establishing a nationwide, known organization that has been a tremendous resource for pet

caretakers and animal rescue shelters that seek knowledge and support.

A farmer had dropped Duke off at the shelter we chose to stop at when we decided we wanted to get another pet. I'm guessing he had no idea how special that animal he was letting go of would turn out to be. These days Duke spends a lot of time doing what he loves best—trail walking, beach walking, or just hanging in the backyard with his canine and human family. In the meantime, he helps give pets worldwide a second chance at life. They say what goes around comes around—and if it's Duke in his wheelchair, you better step out of the way!

Skooch

Kelly Smith, Stay-at-Home Mother

Skooch is the best dog anyone could ask for. She was born without her two front legs, and her mother, Tigger, never treated her differently and loved her just as much as the other puppies. From the get-go, Skooch was extremely active and so most nights we found ourselves constantly having to place her back at her mother's side because she would tend to roll away and was unsure how to make her way back.

I knew my parents would never be able to find someone who was willing to buy a purebred Dachshund without front legs and I certainly didn't have the heart to leave her. You see, Skooch and I share a special connection: I, too, was born with birth defects of my shoulder and spine—so Skooch's determination and spirit won me over instantly. We became inseparable.

When Skooch was four weeks old, my future husband and I were traveling through the mountains of Alaska on our way to Canada. We were goofing around and howling and, as if on cue, Skooch joined right in with us. It was the cutest thing I had ever seen. Soon we decided to stop in a grassy area in Canada to eat some lunch and stretch our legs. At this point, Skooch still hadn't figured out how to move around—she could get around a small area, like her bed, but was unable to move any distance. We figured eventually we would have to get her fitted for a wheelchair. Apparently we were wrong.

I placed Skooch about five feet away, out of curiosity, to see what she would do, or if she was capable of coming over to me. Skooch has two small chicken-winglike appendages where her legs should be, and she sat in the grass wiggling and trying as hard as she could. I was about to go pick her  up when, out of pure will, she began to hop on her chest—using her wings to pull her along. That's when we decided to name her Skooch and since then nothing has stopped her from getting where she wants to go.

Today Skooch hops her way all over the yard and loves to chase squirrels and other dogs. When she was younger she could even hop onto the furniture to curl up on my lap. Now that she's older, she has slowed down a bit—hopping to her destination but then getting up onto her hind legs and wiggling her chicken wings until someone picks her up and places her on the couch. We tried to put her in a homemade doggy wheelchair but she didn't like it at all. In typical Skooch fashion, she thought the chair held her back.

Skooch truly is amazing and greatly loved by everyone in my family. She's definitely one of a kind and will be deeply missed when she passes on. But for now, she's still brightening the lives of everyone who gets the chance to meet her. She's a living inspiration and she taught me a lesson in love—one of many in this life. Legs or no legs, no matter what, I'll love her unconditionally.

Auggie and Aggie

Connie Castanera, Board/Committee Volunteer; Tim Harrison,
Chief Operating Officer, National Cathedral, Washington, DC

Auggie came into our life in October of 1994. We picked him out from a litter of nine Labrador retrievers. He had the shiniest coat of all the ten-week-old puppies. Shortly after bringing him home, we began to notice that Auggie would run into walls and often miscalculate how much room there was to turn around in the hallway as he played with his toys. I really became suspicious that he could be blind when I bounced a ball and he didn't catch it with accuracy. He seemed to miss it most of the time.

At first I thought he was just a klutzy puppy. I tested his vision by passing my hand over each of his eyes. I concluded that he was completely blind in his right eye, could at best see shadows from his left eye, and apparently had bad cataracts in both. Although I felt bad for him at the time, there was no way that I would trade him in for any other dog. Auggie had a home with us and we wouldn't have it any other way.

Not long after I had discovered that he was blind, the breeder called to inform us that most of the other puppies in the litter were blind too and had a condition known as "dwarfism." Typically, with this condition, they have detached retinas and their front legs are either somewhat malformed or shorter than their back legs. Auggie had "bulldog" front legs and was blind, but otherwise he was normal in every other way. The breeder called to let us know that she wasn't aware that the father of the puppies had dwarfism in his breeding line; she was never informed by the owner. The breeder offered to take Auggie back, plus give us a full refund, but there was no way we would ever have given up on Auggie. He was now part of our family.

My husband, Tim, and I agreed that he had the best personality and was the smartest dog that either one of us had ever had. Auggie was almost human—funny, playful, lovable, and very food motivated. He would do anything for food. We would dress him up, pose him, and tell him to "stay," and he would freeze in place. As soon as he heard the click of the camera he'd shake off whatever we dressed him up in. He knew that he was going to get his payoff. Auggie didn't work for free.

If we turned the lights out at bedtime and continued to talk, he would tell us to shut up in his own way—take in a deep breath and release it with a long, dramatic  moan. If that didn't work, he would get up and reposition himself in his bed, while moaning longer and louder than ever. After much laugher, we eventually quieted down so that he could get a peaceful night's rest.

Once while visiting a friend out of state who had a Lab-mix female named Dyna (whom Auggie adored), he did the funniest thing he had ever done. Dyna was chewing a bone that Auggie wanted, so he gave us the signal that he needed to go outside—by pacing back and forth and whining by the door. When our friend opened the door to let him out, Auggie ran toward the door but didn't go outside; instead he hid in the bathroom, knowing that Dyna would head out to join him outside. Dyna stopped chewing the bone and ran out to join Auggie in the yard, as he predicted she would. As Dyna ran outside, Auggie ran for the bone. We couldn't believe that he had tricked her into going out so that he could take it from her. Everyone broke into laughter as Auggie sat there, chomping away on his new toy.

Auggie had multiple medical issues, but it never stopped him from being happy, funny, lovable, and the best companion we ever had. One day, Auggie started to get bloated and had to have emergency surgery to flip his stomach back and tack it down so that it wouldn't happen again. As he got older, he became epileptic, experiencing three to five seizures a year. He also developed

glaucoma in his right eye, which caused his eye to grow abnormally large and turn completely red. We took him to a specialist who removed his eye and inserted a prosthetic one.

The last several months of his precious life, he began to exhibit odd behavior—like walking in circles around our kitchen table. And not just a few circles, he would walk for at least half an hour. Or he would walk into a corner of the room and not know how to get out. He began to get more and more confused about his surroundings.

I did some research on the Internet and concluded that he had canine cognitive dysfunction, which means "doggy Alzheimer's disease." The veterinarian confirmed my theory and we put him on medication. While the medicine helped some, Auggie was eleven and a half years old and soon his condition began progressing rapidly. He didn't know who we were, where he was, or where to relieve himself. The worst part was that he was blind and started bumping into everything that got in his way. We knew we had to make a decision at that point to spare him the torture he was going through, and that was the most difficult decision either of us ever had to make. We took him to the vet and had him put to sleep. My husband and I cried for weeks. It was so difficult to live without our precious Auggie. He had brought so much joy into our lives. Healthy or sick, we adored him and when he left us, he left a huge hole in our hearts as well.

I told my husband that I didn't want another dog, but he knew I wouldn't be happy being "dogless," so after a few weeks he started surfing the Internet in search of other black Labs that needed homes. After finding a Web site that rescues Labrador retrievers, I agreed to take a look at it. One of the dogs, a female Lab that looked like Auggie, caught our eye, and as we read her description, we were amazed to see that this dog's name was Aggie and she was also blind, due to dwarfism! The site also mentioned that adoption time could take up to eight weeks and so I felt discouraged and didn't want to apply.

A few weeks went by and after visiting a local shelter with no luck, we decided to go back to that Web site to see if Aggie was still available—she was. I called the phone number that was listed and explained that we had just lost Auggie and that we knew exactly what we would be getting into, having already had a blind dog. Several days later, Liz, the woman who had rescued Aggie from the shelter, brought Aggie to us with a new crate, toys, food, treats, and her recent medical records.

Aggie had been found in the middle of the street in Virginia. She was sitting there, leaning against another dog that had been hit and killed by a car. The man who found her put her in his car and took her to a local shelter. She was there for about two weeks, and was about to be put to sleep because of overcrowded conditions, when Lab rescue workers took her out of the shelter. Liz, Aggie's foster caretaker, kept her for five months until we found them.

Today, Aggie lives with us on our fifty-two-acre farm and seems to be as happy to be with us as we are to have her as our new companion. She takes daily walks with us and gets daily back rubs and belly rubs from my husband and me. We don't know who named her Aggie, but it was meant for her to have a name that would draw our attention to her. From Auggie to Aggie, with blindness as the common bond, we don't mind being seeing-eye people. As the saying goes, love is blind.

Blanche

Ed Farrell, Retired Surveyor (Told by Joyce Darrell)

It was going to be a hot summer scorcher outside so I began my daily routine jog early in the morning to beat the heat. Pounding the soft ground, no sooner had I gotten into a runner's groove, I was startled by a medium-sized dog lying quietly at the edge of the woods. I came to a halt and hesitated a moment before approaching her.

She warily kept her eyes on me and I looked her over with the same amount of caution. She appeared to be a mangy shepherd mix of some sort. Immediately she reminded me very much of the dog I grew up with when I was a child. I crouched down to get a better look at her and it was obvious that she was hungry, thirsty, and in desperate need of some much-needed human kindness. Rising slowly to not startle her, I reversed direction and headed back home to get my husband.

When I got to the house, the phone had already been ringing off the hook. Word got around that there was a rabid dog on the loose and the neighborhood was working itself into a frenzy. I tried to assure everyone that the dog outside was definitely not rabid—that she was just exhausted, starved, and dehydrated. They remained skeptical.

To stop everyone from worrying, I decided to call our local animal control center, and workers went out and retrieved her from where I saw her last. As soon as I hung up the phone, I began wondering what would happen to the scruffy dog, and my heart started to ache for her in a way I didn't think possible for an animal I had only seen once. I started thinking about how she was probably locked in a small crate, being neglected by humans, once again, who had let her down when all she wanted was to be loved. My eyes welled up with tears and I knew I had to find her.

The next day, we went to the animal shelter where she was being held, signed the necessary paperwork and paid the fees, and lovingly embraced her as our own. And then we took her to the veterinarian's office . . .

The poor pup was riddled with heartworms. She was extremely weak and could barely stand. Because she was in such poor condition, there was no way she would be able to undergo heartworm treatment. To make matters more complicated, the vet told us that she was totally deaf in both ears too. We also had no idea of telling how old she was because all of her teeth were missing. Perhaps she had once been chained to a fence and had chewed her way off of it and was on the run ever since, away from whatever hell she had been enduring. We weren't entirely sure what her story was but what we *did* know was that she was in desperate need of some TLC. Unfortunately, since my husband and I work long hours, we realized we weren't going to be able to give her the undivided attention she needed. Luckily, we knew just the right man who could.

Ed Farrell, a retired surveyor and one of the world's rare, kind souls, didn't hesitate for a moment when we explained our situa-

tion to him. He eagerly took
her in and fittingly named
her "Blanche," after Blanche
Dubois—a character in *A
Streetcar Named Desire*—who
depended entirely on the
kindness of strangers. We
all took turns making daily
gourmet meals of chicken
or beef and rice for our new
friend, Blanche, and spoiled
her as much as possible.
We marveled at how strong

Blanche was getting and how her spirits seemed to brighten a
little bit more each day. She even became friends with Buddy,
Ed's big Lab mix, and soon became Buddy's shadow—hardly ever
leaving his side.

It was such a huge reward to see Blanche feeling better and
playing the way a dog should be able to play, but soon her rough
life caught up with her and she passed away at Ed's home. It was
a terribly sad and emotional day for all of us, especially for our
friend, Ed. Looking back now, though, we are able to smile whole-
heartedly knowing that we gave her the best days we could have
given her since the morning she was found by the woods.

Soon after, Ed passed away as well. He will be greatly missed
by everyone who knew him—he was one of those kindhearted
guys who always put others before himself, especially his dogs. I'm
sure Ed and Blanche are happy, healthy, and living it up together
somewhere in a better place.

Oreo

*Birgit Aviles, Treasurer of the West End Shelter
in Ontario, California*

Puppies get dropped off at our shelter all the time. However, when a beautiful seven-week-old, black-and-white puppy was brought to us by a Good Samaritan one day, everyone in the building instantly fell in love with her. She was so small and  helpless, we all took turns holding her and were eager to find her a deserving home. Oreo seemed to be an appropriate name because of her coloring and because of how sweet and even tempered she was.

Looking closely though, we noticed something was terribly wrong with her hind legs. We took her to several specialists who all confirmed the same thing: her spinal cord never fused properly in utero. This meant that she would never be able to use her back legs and most likely would always be incontinent. Fortunately, they told us, this adorable little pointer puppy felt no pain despite her situation.

Oreo has an amazing spirit and is always scooting around the shelter yelping and playing with all the other pups. She hardly realizes she's "different"—in fact, in lots of ways she's not. And to make Oreo's life a little easier, one day another Good Samaritan came into our shelter with a custom-made wheelchair for her. It took her a little while to get used to, but now she is loving life even more. What would make her most happy though is to find a forever home.

Today Oreo is still at our shelter waiting for that special family to open up their hearts to her. Oreo currently resides in our West End office, energetically meeting and greeting potential adopters. Everyone always crouches down to pet her and mention how cute she is, but then they continue on to look at the other available pets. They're unwilling to make the commitment of taking *her* home. But Oreo remains hopeful, always covering people in

slobbery kisses as they walk in. I know there is a person out there willing to take her into his or her family, and give her the extra attention she needs and deserves. In return, Oreo will probably be the most popular dog in that person's neighborhood, paws down.

For information on Oreo, please contact:

Hope for Oreo
West End Shelter
1010 East Mission Boulevard
Ontario, California 91761
909-947-3517
Web site: www.westendshelter.org

Ava

Ashley Merker, Student/Teacher's Assistant

It was the fall of 2004 and I decided I was ready to adopt a dog of my own. My good friend, Danielle, had e-mailed me a link to a Web site called Petfinder.com that she had come across while surfing the Internet. I figured this would be a good place to start and so I checked it out.

Browsing through all the different advertisements, I somehow managed to come across a listing for a little white puppy born without eyes—she was completely blind. Her story intrigued me and I wanted to learn more about her.

I traveled to the shelter where she was located, and the shelter staff, extremely courteous and friendly, told me that this puppy had been abandoned in a cardboard box, along with her sister and two brothers—one of whom was born with only one eye. The veterinarian at the shelter had contemplated putting the puppy without eyes to sleep, fearing she would never be able to find a permanent home. With a little perseverance from the shelter staff and promises to the vet that they would do everything in their effort to find her a family, the puppy's life was saved.

After hearing her story, I was so excited to meet her and when a staff member brought me to where she was kept, I couldn't help but

smile. She was adorable. I'm not sure how she knew I was there but she didn't hesitate to come right up to me when I offered her my hand. She even started playfully chewing my finger with her tiny teeth. Enjoying the attention, she proceeded to roll over onto her back so that I could scratch her belly. It was undeniable— instantly I was in love. I no longer thought about her not having any eyes; I just looked at her as a shelter puppy that needed a good home. A week later I adopted her and named her Ava.

Training Ava, for the most part, was a breeze. Inevitably, she had her fair share of bumping into furniture at first but now she has learned to navigate her way around her home with ease. She absolutely loves playing with children, other dogs, and, of course, her toys. I love Ava so much and I cannot imagine my life without her. She is the perfect dog for me.

Daisy

Tracey Eno, Massage Therapist;
Laura Magdeburger, Marine Biologist

Laura had seen the tiny three-legged puppy earlier in the day. It was my turn to "go take a look." We had decided it was best to go separately. That way, we couldn't be talked into taking the dog if we weren't interested. "I'll have to go home and talk it over with Laura," I'd say strategically.

As I pulled into the driveway, I could hear the sound of barking dogs. The owner greeted me at the kitchen door and invited me past his pack of five Jack Russell terriers. He had heard about this special Jack puppy and figured he could take her. But she was so tiny—just seven weeks old—and he thought she would do better in a quieter home. He thought of us.

There she was with her little black head and big floppy ears— and three good legs. The fourth leg, her front right one, was only a stump. She was born this way. The breeder had taken her to the vet to be put down, but the vet had refused, saying she was perfectly healthy. But I wondered . . . *Was there anything else wrong with her? Would the stump have to be amputated? Could she get around OK? Would taking her mean lots of medical bills?*

Who was I kidding? She was too adorable to pass up. Totally discarding "the plan," I decided to follow my heart and told the man we'd take her. It was February—a cold, windy, and snowy night—so I tucked her inside my coat, with her tiny head sticking out near my own, and took her home.

I suppose Laura had known all along what I would do. She didn't seem at all surprised when I walked in the door with the little handful of puppy fuzz. Zoe, our three-year-old Jack Russell, sniffed the puppy and seemed to accept the idea of having a sister.

Daisy's three legs soon grew long and strong. The deformed leg (we affectionately call it her "Crab Claw") no longer gets in the way. She smartly positions the front left foot in the middle of her stance, sort of like a wheelbarrow. We lovingly call that good leg her "Big Wheel." Despite her disability, she is extremely active and runs similar to the way a rabbit does—with both hind legs moving together.

Daisy has participated twice in the Jack Russell National Trials in Havre de Grace, Maryland. She ran the obstacle course so fast that most observers didn't even realize her handicap until she crossed the finish line. Aside from competitions, she also has a part-time job working at the Calvert Marine Museum every Monday. As a puppy, she went to work with Laura every day until she was housebroken. Now she continues to go by popular demand. One of her favorite things to do is entertain "the ladies"—the senior museum volunteers who always have puppy treats ready for her. She makes them laugh. At lunchtime, she often goes with Laura through a nearby restaurant drive-through and somehow always manages to sneak a chicken tender.

Today six-year-old Daisy loves to bark at turtles, chase squirrels, dive into Chesapeake Bay, and sleep under the covers at night. All in all, it's a dog's life, really. People sometimes ask, sympathetically, "Aw, what happened to her?" We sort of just laugh and explain that she was born that way but that she doesn't think she's different at all. Then we add, "She often wonders why other dogs have an *extra* leg!"

Huey

*Joyce Darrell, Small Business Owner and
Cofounder of Pets with Disabilities*

It truly amazes me how dogs can bring people together. Through our dogs, my husband, Mike, and I met Lillie Goodrich and John Andersen—a couple who gave up their careers to rescue border collies. They own a whimsical place called Glen Highland Farm, a rescue farm for border collies. The couple invites other dog enthusiasts to enjoy their farm and to help subsidize their rescue efforts.

The farm is acres upon acres of fun for any canine—or human—who visits. Endless leashless opportunities abound: trail walking, swimming in the river, exploring the agility course—all guaranteed good times. When we found out the farm had several trails, we knew the place would be perfect for our feisty, wheelchair-bound dog, Duke. And it was—today, he is obsessed with trail walking.

Over the past few years, we have visited the farm hundreds of times. In the process, our friendship with John and Lillie grew stronger. We formed a mutual admiration for the work we both do in helping dogs—theirs with border collies and ours with disabled dogs. One weekend while visiting, Lillie had a milestone

birthday. We told her that we would adopt a border collie from them as a present from us. There was only one condition: it had to be disabled (because disabled dogs tend to be difficult to place in homes). Never in the world did we think she was actually going to take us up on our offer.

That following month, Lillie sent me an e-mail with the message: *How about a deaf border collie puppy?* She also included a few pictures of the pup as an attachment. Clicking on the images, it was a no-brainer. Mike and I fell in love with him at first sight. We planned another weekend to go visit our friends and bring home Huey. Time couldn't fly by fast enough.

We now understand the whole border collie mystique. Huey's beauty is beyond words—his fur is like silk. Besides being so handsome, he is extremely agile and very bright. For example, with a little time and patience, at the tender age of two months he was learning hand signs. Even though he can't hear anything, he can use his other senses perfectly and he's quite an active dog. It's fun to just sit back and watch him poke around and be curious about the world.

Today I'm almost certain he sleeps with one eye open so that he doesn't miss a thing. I am grateful for the friendship we share with John and Lillie, I am grateful for Huey being a wonderful addition to our family, and I am grateful for the opportunity to be able to help out these amazing animals, one pup at a time.

Darwin

Cindy Vernasco, Founder of Roxie's Fund, Inc., a Rottweiler and Mixed-Breed Rescue Organization; Owner of All Dogs Club, Doggie Day Care, and Cageless Pajama Parties

Less than a year had passed when Darwin, a Rottweiler mix, was brought back to the Pennsylvania animal shelter he had been adopted from. Darwin's unknown disability had progressed and the family who tried to care for him was unable to keep up with his growing needs. When they decided it would be best to return him, he was already unable to walk.

The shelter watched over Darwin for a couple of months. The staff examined him closely and eventually ruled out that he could be an abuse case. No cruelty could be determined. While staying at the shelter, Darwin proved to be an excellent dog—winning over the hearts of every single shelter employee there. Unfortunately, the shelter staff knew they did not have the time or financial means to really help Darwin the way he needed to be helped. That's when they contacted my animal welfare group, Roxie's Fund, Inc., for assistance.

After explaining Darwin's situation and what an incredibly sweet dog he was, there was no hesitation on our part. Immediately, we became committed to getting him the care he desperately needed. I knew we had the resources to help him get a diagnosis and more important—a new home.

After several veterinary office visits, blood work, X-rays, and even a trip to the University of Florida for further evaluation, Darwin was diagnosed with a degenerative nervous system disease known as Rottweiler polyneuropathy. He would need ongoing therapy to build muscle mass and help with his coordination.

In the meantime, we had several families interested in adopting Darwin, but they too came to realize that they did not have the time or energy needed to dedicate to Darwin. That's when

I knew in my heart that Darwin was going to become a part of my family.

Today Darwin is stronger than ever, but he goes to physical therapy once a week. Even though he can't really walk long distances, he tries hard to do so anyway. In the process, he sort of mimics the way a baby colt walks—unsteady and slow—but he is filled with determination. My other five dogs simply adore him and love to play around with him too. When Darwin gets tired, he uses his brother Zoe's back as a buffer to help him lie gently on the floor.

Darwin is an incredible dog with an enormous heart. He's loving life just as he should be. Taking him into my home is a decision I have never regretted. I'm truly blessed to have him in my pack.

Gilbert

Barbara Thrasher, Founder and Director of BONES
(Better Options for Neglected Strays); Debi and Bill Frogue,
Retired Commercial Fishermen

Today I took the two-hour drive with Gilbert to his new home. I had many phone conversations with Debi, Gilbert's new "mom," and I felt confident I was making the right decision. From the look on his face, he seemed to know this too.

When I was first contacted to rescue Gilbert, I learned that he was about a year old and had been abandoned by the caregiver of an elderly woman. She knew that she couldn't give him the attention and care that he needed. Gilbert is a paraplegic with no feeling from his hips on down—so he can't use his back legs at all. The woman I spoke with said she thought he had been stepped on by someone when he was a puppy. Gilbert is a four-and-three-quarter-pound Doxie-terrier mix with beautiful blond fur, big ears, and a very expressive face. In other words, he's absolutely adorable.

When we arrived to rescue him, he began barking fiercely at us and was dragging himself around a litter-strewn yard. There were noticeable sores on his legs and tummy from carrying himself over the dirt and gravel. He was so afraid of us that the woman caring for him had to catch him and put him in the kennel because he didn't want anything to do with us. We covered the kennel with a towel to make him feel more secure. If we even attempted to look under the towel, Gilbert would snap and snarl. This was going to be an interesting day.

Once home, I placed the crate on the floor and opened the door so he could come out when he felt comfortable. I desper-

ately wanted him to know that no one would hurt him ever again—but he still wasn't ready. It was a long process, but as the days passed Gilbert finally began to start to trust me. It wasn't long before we were best friends.

I started taking him with me on errands so that I could socialize him with other people. He was cautious to warm up to strangers but usually would consent to take a treat from them if they moved slowly and didn't try to pet him. The trouble is he's so cute that everyone always wanted to touch him.

Eventually Gilbert became comfortable with me and my other pets and after that was established he turned into a little clown. Whenever he got excited he'd run in a figure-eight pattern around the living room or on the bed. By that time he was also sleeping under the covers and loved to snuggle. I bought some steps so one of my other little old dogs could get up on the bed. To my surprise,

Gilbert learned to get himself up the steps and onto the bed. He was very proud of his accomplishment—and I was, too.

It's funny how things work out. One day, through a friend, I heard about a couple who once had a paraplegic dog and adored her beyond words. Sadly, they lost her to a bone infection after only four years. The thought of maybe finding Gilbert the "perfect" home was exciting. I definitely loved him, but he really wasn't getting the attention that he deserved. (Because of my rescue work my home is always filled to capacity with so many other critters and each one takes a portion of my time.) The possibility of Gilbert getting to have a family of his own was exciting . . . but a little scary at the same time.

After talking at length with Debi many times by phone, I was 100 percent sure that Gilbert would have a wonderful life with her and her husband, Bill. Even before we left, I sensed that Gilbert knew. He started getting really clingy and insisted on being held more often than normal. While I was happy he'd be going to a great new home I was so attached to him that it was difficult to let him go.

Debi and I met at a supermarket parking lot. From the second I introduced the two, Gilbert let her pet him without hesitation. He never did that without at least a few moments of coaxing and reassurance from me—he liked her. I followed Debi to her house and we put Gilbert on the floor. He allowed her to pet him some more and then scooted off to investigate the house. He helped himself to a

drink of water from the kitchen, making himself at home. A little later, I put him in the small wheelchair I had made for him. He was somewhat unsure of the contraption at first, but I was confident he'd get accustomed to his new legs with practice. Finally, we said our bittersweet good-byes, and I headed home as Gilbert began his new life with a wonderful family.

It is difficult to explain to someone who wonders why you would choose a "broken" little critter when there are so many perfect ones out there looking for homes too. All animals are special, but there is something so humbling about a small creature with a disability that asks for nothing but love, and gives it back in multitudes. They never complain about their situation . . . they just live with it and love life. It's truly awe inspiring to be involved with one of these miracle pets. They have spirit and strength that are to be envied.

Bogey

Charlie Di Pietro, Retired Investment Representative;
Bev Di Pietro, Retired Owner of a Specialty Chocolate Business

Bogey creates quite a stir in any RV park my wife, Bev, and I stay at as he walks proudly in his "chariot"—sporting his Harley-Davidson cap and leash or his red, white, and blue visor and matching breeches. People often come out of their RVs to see him up close and meet him. He'll be willing to stop his march only for a moment to say hello to these nice folks, but then he starts chewing and pulling on his leash as if to say, "Let's roll."

Like many RV enthusiasts, Bev and I began taking our small dog with us on every trip we took in our American Eagle coach—which is now called home for this family. However, on one such trip in August 2002 to Reno, Nevada, Bogey, our twelve-pound poodle, developed a problem. Although he was healthy and only five and a half years old at the time, he somehow managed to blow a disk in his back. The complete rear half of his body became paralyzed.

We had to take immediate action. Bev and I took Bogey to a qualified animal clinic in Carson City where we talked to a veterinarian and discussed all of our options. After many examinations, Bogey underwent difficult spinal surgery.

Weeks of recovery time and numerous therapy sessions went by and then it became apparent to us that Bogey would never walk again. We were devastated, but we definitely knew we weren't going to put him down. We searched the Internet and came across Dewey's Wheelchairs for Dogs. The next logical step was to drive to Oregon where the company was located and have a custom wheelchair made for our little trooper.

As soon as Bogey was placed in his wheelchair, there was no hesitation—he took off as fast as his front legs could carry him. Bogey has continued to have that same spark for life as he travels with us throughout the western United States and Canada.

Today, Bogey weighs only eight pounds, but his front end has become extremely strong. While inside our coach he manages to get around quite well without his wheelchair. He scoots along with ease on the smooth tile flooring, but we have to lift him up to his favorite spot on the couch. He learned very quickly how to ask to be put up on the couch, bed, or our laps by a sharp, demanding bark. It works every time.

A few years have passed since Bogey's accident, but he doesn't seem to think there's anything different with him than before. He loves traveling with us and we have shared so many good times on the road. Our motor home license plate reads ROLNON ("rolling on") and we plan to continue seeking great new adventures along the road with our little buddy, Bogey.

Mikey

Carol Kelly, retired writer/editor
(Told by Ann Selnick, President of Animal Advocates
of Howard County, Maryland)

Over two years ago, Animal Advocates of Howard County (AAHC) received a desperate phone call from a cat rescuer who noticed an adorable little poodle mix dragging his hind legs around in someone's backyard. It was very sad and obvious that the dog needed immediate medical attention. The cat rescuer suspected a family member had abused the dog for some time. AAHC agreed to help Mikey, but only if the owners gave up custody of the poor pup. And so began Mikey's wonderful new life.

Staff members from AAHC rushed him to the vet where the doctors determined that his injuries were so severe and long term that they feared he would never walk again. Mikey would probably have to use a wheelchair for the rest of his life. Mikey was brought to a local boarding home for dogs where almost immediately the staff there fell in love with him. He won them over with his vivacious and indomitable spirit.

It took some time, but the shelter staff collected donations and chipped in money of their own to purchase a wheelchair for

Mikey. After that, the search was on for a new and forever home for the little guy.

Pets with Disabilities invited Mikey and AAHC to participate in a charity dog walk where Mikey could possibly encounter a potential adoptive family. At that walk a match was made in heaven.

Mikey's future mom was strolling by the Pets with Disabilities booth when Mikey caught her eye. He was busy happily flirting with everyone who stopped to meet him. Carol Kelly, a Capitol Hill retiree, decided to adopt Mikey on the spot. A self-proclaimed "cat person," she knew she still had plenty of room in her heart and home to take on this loving ball of fuzz, despite his disability.

Today Mikey is the pied piper of Capitol Hill. He proudly cruises the streets—stopping traffic, greeting old friends, and constantly meeting new ones. He has become somewhat of a celebrity in the neighborhood. But above all, he has become an educator on the importance of humane treatment for all pets. While Carol still loves her felines, she proved that cat lovers can be dog lovers too, doggone it!

Jackie

*Tanya Lichterman, Education Coordinator/
Special Education Teacher*

"She's blind," she told me. "If you get a chance, please go visit her. She needs some extra attention." It was the summer of 2003 and my friend, Carol, who heads an animal rescue group, wanted me to go see a Jack Russell terrier that was being boarded at a local kennel until she found a home. At the time I was pre-occupied with the terminal illness of my beloved poodle, Rusty, and so I passed up the offer.

A week after Rusty passed away, Carol came to visit me. She said that since she was in the area she was going to make a special stop to see the little blind dog and asked if I wanted to go along. We both *knew* there were ulterior motives to her question and I found myself agreeing to go—as long as my mother, the voice of reason, came along too. I was aware that I probably wasn't ready to make any sound decision since it was so soon after Rusty's death. The three of us met at the kennel.

Being a special education teacher, I was prepared for the fact that this dog didn't have any eyes—I honestly didn't give that part too much thought. After all, every creature is unique in its own way. Carol scooped up the dog and the four of us went outside to see how she'd behave.

Once in the fresh air, the little dog immediately sat down in the grass. Oddly, she seemed depressed and sad. The sun was shining and a warm breeze was blowing, but all the dog did was tilt her sightless face to the sky and let out the biggest sigh a dog her size could muster. At that moment, my mother pointed to the parking lot and very firmly—as only a mother can do—said, "Get in the car. Take that dog home, right now!" And so began Jackie's life with me. It just felt right.

Given my teaching background, I was able very naturally to make accommodations for my new friend. I put plastic runners on the carpet in strategic walkways, laid out rugs of various textures leading to the back door, put an outdoor carpet in the yard leading back to the door from the outside, and easily began to make it a habit of not moving furniture, not leaving shoes or other items in the middle of the floor, and not allowing others to do so either. When I would take her on walks, I would wear a bracelet of bells around my ankle so she would be able to hear wherever I went.

I watch in amazement as Jackie approaches and then easily avoids obstacles she has never encountered before. It was almost as if she began to somehow sense that things were in front of her before I could even tell her. One day I was reading an article that noted that people with visual impairments can be taught to *echo-locate* to help them navigate around obstacles, in the way that a

bat or dolphin uses sonar. It was then that I realized Jackie must be using her "extra sense" to maneuver through her environment.

Many parts of Jackie's history remain a mystery to me, but I was told a few details from her past. She grew up with horses and was kicked by one—possibly the cause of the need to remove her eyes. The accident with the horse, however, is more likely the cause of her back and hip deformities. Little Jackie had many owners in her lifetime—kind people who heard of her plight and offered to take her in. After being told, "No pets allowed," another neighbor, who couldn't bear to see her put out, took her in. It was this neighbor's friend who offered to pay for Jackie's eye surgery. I was told her eyes were shriveled like raisins and were very painful for her.

Like other owners of blind dogs, I've encountered numerous people over the years who are curious about her blindness. I'm often asked, "Are you *sure* she can't see?" They ask this question because they somehow don't think a blind dog can get around as well as she does. They seem to be amazed when I respond, "She has no eyes. Yes, I'm pretty sure she can't see." Recently, at the veterinarian's office, a man asked me, "Does she know where she is?" Given that Jackie, like many other pets, isn't a fan of going to the doctor, I chuckled and replied, "Oh yes. She is *very* aware of where she is!"

Living with Jackie is definitely not without its challenges. Because of her true Jack Russell nature, combined with her difficult and painful history, she continues to startle easily when she's asleep—often snapping and occasionally biting me or anything else in her path. She also barks at things I neither hear nor see because her hearing abilities are so sensitive. When we go for walks, she'll bark for reasons unknown to me—and then I'll see someone coming down the street a few minutes later. Jackie is also aggressive toward other animals, so after my other dog passed away, she continues to be an only child.

My family and friends no longer see Jackie as a dog with a disability, often forgetting she has no eyes. After discussing the possibility of purchasing a carrier for Jackie to ride in on outings, a friend of mine inquired how Jackie would react if she saw another dog through the mesh sides of the basket. She caught herself in midthought, realizing what she just said. Jackie has taught others to see beyond her differences, to celebrate her unique nature, and to be more aware that pets and people with disabilities are just like everybody else.

Despite all of Jackie's issues—she now also suffers from medical concerns associated with old age—I love her very much and as each day passes I'm more and more amazed at her strength and will to overcome her daily challenges. Besides, who needs eyes? After all, what they say is true: blind dogs see with their hearts.

Misty

*Renee Boockvor, Executive Director of Westchester County
Humane Society; Joyce Darrell, Small Business Owner
and Founder of Pets with Disabilities*

RENEE: We received a phone call about a young pup that had been possibly hit by a car. Immediately, the staff at Westchester County Humane Society went to check out the situation. As soon as we saw her, we agreed that she had been hit: she was dragging the back half of her tiny body. It was absolutely heartbreaking.

We had our vets examine her and found out that the puppy was actually born without any hip sockets. Instead of caring for her, someone decided it'd be much easier to simply dump the disabled puppy on the side of the road. We decided to call her Misty and hoped that her story would tug at someone's heartstrings and she would be adopted soon and loved unconditionally.

It wasn't quite that easy. Days went by . . . then months . . . then years—five years to be exact. But one day out of the blue I received the phone call I had been waiting forever for. Someone was interested in little Misty.

* * *

JOYCE: It was a cold January day and I was just reopening my business after a big snowstorm had hit the Mid-Atlantic area. I had been shoveling snow for a while and I was tired so I decided to take a break and check the mailbox. Glancing over the usual bills, advertisements, and junk mail, I noticed an envelope from Katonah, New York—my old stomping grounds.

Throwing the bills aside, I opened this letter from a former neighbor, Lois Fritz, trying to imagine why she was contacting me after so many years. Inside the envelope I found a newspaper clipping about cats with disabilities. Could this old neighbor have heard about our disabled dog, Duke? As I read the article, my eyes stopped on a snippet in the very last paragraph about a dog named Misty that used a wheelchair. Misty, the article stated, had been living at the shelter for over five years but had finally found her forever home.

I quickly called the shelter to see if I could talk with Misty's new caretakers. I thought, *Finally, here is another person to chat with about caring for a wheelchair dog!* Not so fast. I got in touch with Renée, the shelter manager, and she furiously informed me that the newspaper had made a horrible mistake. Misty was still in her shelter and still in need of a good home. As I hung up the phone, I looked at Duke, and within minutes my husband, Michael, Duke, and I were piled in the car and headed to New York to meet Misty.

We were already used to taking care of a seventy-pound paralyzed shepherd and figured that caring for a twenty-five-pound disabled dog would be a walk in the park. With Misty, we'd have two spokesdogs to help our Pets with Disabilities cause and spread the word that disabled animals make great pets. From the moment we saw Misty, we knew she was a perfect match for us.

Since Misty has become a spokesdog for our organization, there have been so many people wanting to adopt our little girl. It's kind of a twist of fate for Misty, considering she was a shelter mutt for over five years. Her demeanor is wonderful. She absolutely adores attention and is accepting of all people—adults and children, male or female. Thinking about her and what she's been through sort of makes *me* misty. We're so happy we found out about her on a fluke. She deserves to be in a loving home, without cages, surrounded by people who want to see her happy. And that's what she found.

Jinx

Jan Sapp, Meeting and Conference Planner, PetConnect, Inc.

If you tried to tell Jinx she was disabled because she only has one front leg, she would prove you wrong. She would excitedly show you how high she can jump and how fast she can run. She would show you that she can do anything she wants to do, and then some. She would make you think differently about dogs with disabilities.

When Jinx was about six months old, she and Gypsy, her littermate, were dumped in a field on the fairly remote grounds of an agricultural research center in Maryland. However, in that area bluebird nest box trails were monitored by different people throughout the summer. It was on one of those drives that the puppies were discovered.

Jinx and Gypsy had built a little den in the grass by a stream, which fortunately ran close to a service road. At the sound of the research worker's car nearing, both dogs charged out of their home, barking and growling ferociously. The driver, herself the owner of a menagerie of cats and dogs, stopped the car and approached the fearless bits of fur—but they promptly ran back to their hiding spot. With a little coaxing, Gypsy finally jumped into the woman's car, but there was no persuading Jinx.

Daylight began to fade and she didn't want to leave one dog alone so she let Gypsy out of her car, dashed home for food and fresh water, and hoped they would stay in the same location overnight. The next morning, she rushed to where the puppies were and was happy to see they had stayed put. Even better, both dogs were eager to jump into her car. As the woman drove away from the field, she was sure they'd find much better homes than where she had found them.

She was right. Jinx and Gypsy were brought to a rescue shelter and found new families—Gypsy with a family that taught her that she doesn't have to be afraid of people any longer, and Jinx with me. Jinx is still cautious at times with people and she's clearly the boss of the house but disabled? Not Jinx. After all, she is the instigator of all the fun and mischief in the family!

Saffron

Paul LaRocca, New York Police Department Detective

May 7, 1999. That day, among a few others, has been a life changer. I was driving home along South Avenue on a rainy Friday afternoon when I noticed a police car on the side of the road. I looked more closely to the right and what I saw made me stop immediately and offer my help.

A Port Authority of New York and New Jersey police officer was standing near an injured dog in the bushes alongside the road. The officer was attempting to prevent this small brown dog—a pit bull—from heading back onto South Avenue. The dog was sitting awkwardly, with her legs spread out in front of her, instead of tucked beneath her bottom. When I got out of my car, I saw that portions of the dog's tail, hind legs, and feet were raw with blood—the fur and skin had been scraped off from dragging herself around. She also had two broken teeth, which would eventually have to come out, and 115 ticks all over her body: in her ears, in her snout, and on her rear end. The poor little dog looked like she was at death's door.

We decided to call the dog Saffron and took her to the local animal hospital where two other guys and I split the cost of her initial care. However, when they heard that Saff was permanently

paralyzed because of a broken vertebra they eventually bowed out of the picture. But me, I couldn't give up on this cute pit bull. I had grown too attached to her.

After finding out Saff was paralyzed, I went online and searched the Internet for doggie wheelchairs. I found one that would work for her, and the vets and I gave it a go. It was decent—it got her around. She was finally able to run again and people at the animal hospital got a kick out of seeing her run in the parking lot. I tried to get her adopted—my intentions were never to take her home—but everyone who saw her always seemed to shy away. No one had the time she needed in order to be taken care of properly.

So I did what I had to do. I continued going to the vet after work every day, and went there on weekends to walk her too.

She'd get so excited when she saw me stroll in and when I put her into her wheelchair. We'd walk for a while and then I'd put down a blanket so that she could rest a bit in the sun, and then we'd walk some more. Saff especially loved the weekends. We'd go out all day in the park. People were constantly approaching us. I'd casually bring up that she was available for adoption, but that's when they'd all shy away. I finally came to the conclusion that I would just take her home to my small place with me. My family was totally against it—especially because she was a pit bull—but she was so sweet and all she wanted was her belly to be rubbed. It took a little while, but she eventually won their hearts over too.

After six long months at the vet, Saff finally came home with me. She seemed relieved to be in a quiet and peaceful place away from all the barking and noise from the other animals at the hospital. I'll admit it was tough in the beginning, but once a routine was established, I knew everything would be OK. I bought diapers and little blue jeans pants to place on Saff so that if she were to have an accident, the diapers would come in handy. Were there ever any accidents? Yeah, you bet. In fact, some were whoppers—but it wasn't her fault; I knew she couldn't help it.

Seven years later, Saff is doing excellent. She's now a healthy forty-seven pounds of muscle and still enjoys her power walks at the park where she'll sometimes try to chase squirrels, rabbits, and birds. Saff has been with me through some pretty tough times in my life, always flopping over on her back to let me scratch her belly and help me forget about whatever is stressing me out at the time. She was there for me when my mom died, when I would come home from those cold nights walking a foot post, or just if I'd had a crappy day. She'll see me, know what kind of mood I'm in, and simply flop over. Saff is definitely comedic relief. The tap dance she does at the kitchen table when she's looking for steak is hysterical, and when she sits and stares, longingly, at the turkey in the oven on Thanksgiving? That's pretty funny too.

Saff has taught me so much about patience, compassion, and persistence. Other people seem to learn something from her too when they see us walking around town. I get a lot of head nods and smiles from strangers, but I didn't take her in for the attention or for their kind words—I did it for a little pit bull that someone gave up on.

I read in a book somewhere that animals are our guardian angels. I know that Saff is definitely mine. She is one of the best gifts the universe has given to me. All people should have a Saff in their life. It would make them that much better.

Bruce

Beth Kilmer, President of Chesapeake Shepherd & K-9 Rescue, Inc.;
Hank Kilmer, President of an Internet Consulting Company

I followed the care technician past run after run in a local shelter. We were looking for two dogs I had been called to evaluate, and she suddenly stopped in front of one particular run.

"I want to show you this one, too . . ." she said slowly.

Ugh, I thought, *I don't even have room in my rescue for the two I'm here to see.* "This is Bruce," she said, looking over at me and then back down at the little ball of fur before us. "He's been here two months—someone left him here. We really love him and don't want to euthanize him but we're full. He's ten months old." I looked long and hard at the poor guy.

"Do you think you can help him?" she asked hopefully. And then, without skipping a beat, she added, "He's blind and deaf."

He's blind and deaf? I thought to myself in disbelief. I took a deep breath but then found myself asking the technician to take him out of the pen. I watched him catch my scent and put his paws up on the chain link door. The technician unlatched the gate and out came one of the cutest puppies I've ever seen: an adorable Brittany spaniel and boxer mix. A huge smile spread across my

face. I didn't have a *clue* what I was going to do with him—but I knew I wasn't going to leave him there to die.

As I drove home with him in the back of my car, the wheels in my brain started turning. I wasn't sure how I was going to break the news to my husband, Hank, who was at home waiting for me to get him so we could go visit some former adopters, Joyce Darrell and Michael Dickerson, at a companion animal show.

I pulled into the driveway and parked the car. Hank, looking completely exhausted, climbed in the vehicle without so much as even glancing in the backseat at the puppy. (He wasn't like this all the time. If fact, he has always been a willing and active participant in our rescue, Chesapeake Shepherd & K-9 Rescue, Inc., but it is terribly draining and difficult work most of the time, and Hank was visibly burned out.)

"Don't you want to say hi to him? His name is Bruce," I said, hoping Hank would instantly fall in love with the pup the way I had already done.

"No, let's just get going," he mumbled.

An hour later, we arrived at the show. We met with Michael and Joyce and visited with their dogs for a while—one of whom they had adopted from us earlier in the year—and then started checking out the booths.

Poor Bruce! We accidentally walked him into poles, trash cans, and unsuspecting pet show patrons—just about everyone and everything you can imagine. Unfortunately, we had no experience being seeing-eye humans, so we decided to designate Hank as Bruce's babysitter for the rest of the afternoon. Hank would stay put with Bruce while Joyce and I continued to walk around the show. Later on, I returned to the booth to see a look of bliss on my husband's face as if to say, "Can we keep him?"

Thus began an awe-inspiring spiritual connection between man and his best friend. Even now, Hank is the only one who can soothe Bruce if he gets upset, the only one who can clearly read his moods and tell what he's thinking, and the only one who knows how to make him perfectly content. I have watched in amazement as he simply lays a hand on Bruce and Bruce settles down and relaxes almost immediately.

It took a lot of time and commitment, but eventually we were able to teach Bruce touch signals: sit, "look" down to find something, turn right, turn left, turn about face, step up, and step down. Bruce, in exchange, has taught us about pure love, pure joy, and the pure essence of dog. Everything he does is a result of his inborn instincts, as he couldn't see or hear to model other dogs' behaviors before.

Today, Bruce is able to bravely navigate his home and yard. He confidently explores new environments without fear or hesitation. Bruce is our daily inspiration, and an amazing ambassador for our rescue work. Our little social butterfly charms the crowds at all of our adoption events and teaches everyone he meets about perseverance and overcoming any kind of disability, large and small. He welcomes all of our new foster dogs into the house, and sees it as his personal mission to get them to play and enjoy life again. Whenever we grow weary from our work, all we have to do is look at Bruce—and he rescues us!

Bianca

Kristin Cooper, Humane Society of Harrisburg Area, Pennsylvania

Growing up, I've always had dogs and cats, so when I started working at the Humane Society of Harrisburg Area three years ago, I figured that would be a great place for me. Although I worked with these wonderful animals on a daily basis, I never considered adopting a dog, simply because I rent my place and I know how expensive and stressful owning a dog can be. That is, until one of our dogs gave birth to a special little pure-white female American pit bull terrier. She was beautiful.

There seemed to be a problem though. Of all the puppies born, this one was the lone survivor and for some reason she didn't want to eat and didn't develop well. The onsite vet quickly put her on antibiotics and gave her daily penicillin shots to try and help the poor pup grow stronger. Unfortunately, with so many animals to care for at the shelter, the staff found it difficult to cater to this baby's every need. Without hesitation, I offered to foster her without any intentions of adoption.

I took the puppy home with me every night, making sure she always had her meds and lots of love. Slowly, I watched her grow and learn how to climb stairs. She was constantly getting into everything. She would observe me a lot, learning my facial expressions, and trotting alongside me wherever I went. It was almost like having a small child. She'd sleep on my chest with her little paw lying gently on my face or she would watch me until I dozed off. There was just something about her—I had never met a dog with such a huge personality.

Eventually, the morning came where she was strong enough to go back to the shelter. She was about three months old then and for some reason I was terribly upset about bringing her back. I hadn't planned on falling in love with the little girl, but I did. I knew someone would soon adopt her and provide her with an extraordinary home—but I still didn't want to give her up so suddenly.

She stayed behind the scenes for a while so that the onsite vet and the rest of the staff could observe her and see how she interacted with the other dogs. It was interesting to watch her mingle with the other shelter pups. She never came when called and when she was tired she'd simply go off on her own and fall asleep.

When someone would call to her to wake up, she wouldn't move. We figured she had simply overexerted herself to the point of complete exhaustion, but deep down we were a little concerned.

Upon further investigation we realized this little pup was deaf. Then we got worried. Who would want to adopt a deaf dog? Would she be able to be trained? What kind of life would she end up living? These thoughts raced through my mind over and over again until I couldn't stand it any longer. All I kept picturing was a beautiful puppy growing up to be a hoodlum, without any guidance or sense of purpose, living with a family who just didn't care.

So I named her Bianca and gave in and adopted her myself. Raising Bianca was a breeze. She already knew everything through my facial expressions and hand signals. After four months she was completely crate trained and never had an accident in my house.

Today she knows the commands "sit," "shake," "speak" (yes, deaf dogs bark!), "down," "roll over," "stay," and "do your pretty" (the Bianca dance where she stands on her back legs and jumps in a circle). She has also mastered how to open the refrigerator and serve guests soda or water. She can even put her toys in her toy box after she's through playing with them.

People can hardly believe the obstacles she has overcome. It's hard for me to believe, too. Like a mother, I'm just so proud of my baby girl. She is the smartest, funniest, most lovable dog I have ever known and I wouldn't trade her love for all the money in the world. She's so strong and spirited—an absolute inspiration every day. She has taught me that just because she is different doesn't mean that she can't learn just as much as all the others who don't have disabilities, and that pit bulls make great pets just as Labs and shepherds, or any other dog for that matter. Bianca deserves the best life that I can offer her and I have every intention on delivering that.

Bear

Laura Phillips, Hair Stylist; Gary Phillips, Locksmith

Bear came into our lives in the winter of 1996. He was cold, tired, hungry, very dirty, and collarless. My husband, Gary, found him roaming the streets alone. We tried looking for his owners, but no one ever came forward. It didn't take long for us to embrace Bear, bring him into our family, and give him a forever home.

Bear's appetite seemed to be that of an actual bear. The first few months we had him, he managed to devour everything in sight—including the television remote control, a pair of eyeglasses, numerous articles of clothing, and, of course, our furniture—and then it would seem he was *still* hungry. However, we were patient and loving with him and eventually he became a great family pet.

When Bear turned eleven years old, we took him to the veterinary office and received alarming news: his spine was collapsing and soon he would be unable to use his back legs at all. My husband and I were torn. I wanted Bear to get a wheelchair so that he could enjoy the remainder of his life, playing outside with our other dog and his buddy, Lucky. But my husband seemed very

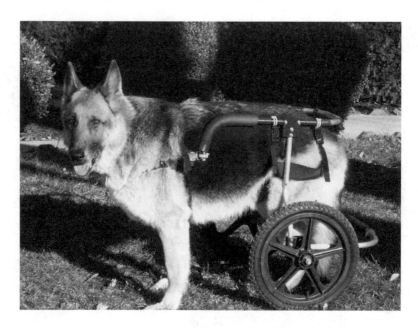

hesitant about putting his German shepherd in a wheelchair. He didn't think it was a good idea.

I was determined. After a little coaxing, I convinced Gary that this was what was needed to be done. Bear was an important part of our family and we had to help him. Oddly, the first wheelchair we ordered never arrived. We were extremely irritated. We had just made a huge decision for Bear, but his wheels never showed up.

By then Gary decided to go on a mission to get his dog a wheelchair. He called up Pets with Disabilities, which was located about two hours away from our home. Gary must've called them ten times in a two-day period. He really wanted what was best for Bear. Coincidentally, the founder of Pets with Disabilities told us that she too had a German shepherd in a wheelchair, and that she had an extra one that Bear could use.

We were so excited that we were in the car, with Bear in tow, the very next day. As soon as we got there and had Bear fitted to the chair, he took off like the wind. It brought tears to our eyes knowing that he could walk and play again. Today, my family is so happy that that we were able to go the extra mile for our Bear. He is a great companion and a true friend.

Rugby, Faith, Mona, Snatch, Tilly, and Grace

Justin Skinner, Student

I may be young, but already some of my life's most important lessons have come in many shapes, sizes, and colors. Their world is one of silence, but they continue to speak in volumes. You see, for the past seven years, I have shared my life with deaf dogs.

My mother has been a dog trainer for over twenty years. She also has a big heart and decided to take in those dogs that others would always overlook: dogs that are deaf. All of these dogs have come either from shelters or the streets. The lucky ones came from responsible breeders. Each one has taught me a lesson about what life has to offer:

Rugby, a deaf English cocker spaniel, taught me to accept the less than perfect. I watched him arrive in this world as an unconnected soul. Then I felt the disappointment of learning of his disability. Time gave me the chance to marvel at the way he adapted to a silent world and became a loving being. He has taught me the value of being different.

Faith, a deaf Dalmatian, taught me the value of forgiveness. She came as a terrified dog. Time, patience, and space taught her to trust humans. From her, I learned to turn a cheek to those who may be cruel or unkind. I have learned that most cruelty is not personal but a lack of moral character in the perpetrator.

Mona taught me to go forward despite struggles that could block one's way. A deaf French bulldog, she suffered from a terminal liver malforma-tion. Regardless, she manages to greet each morning with a lick and a wag. From her, I learned not to whine about life's little dif-ficulties. I learned that perseverance can overcome just about any-thing. We all have hurdles put in our way. Now I just look at them as challenges. Snatch, a deaf bull terrier, taught me to enjoy life. An ant crawling across the floor can become the most entertaining event. A burst of frenetic activity can invigorate the entire body. The simple touch of a human hand can warm the soul. One should take time every day to give thanks for simply being alive. Life may give you obstacles, but there is great pleasure in the process of over-coming them. Tilly, a deaf border collie, taught me there are no disabilities. It's all in the way you approach life. Life is too short and there is too much to do to let life's obstacles slow you down. She goes at everything full speed and with great exuberance. She has taught me to go for what I want and to be persistent. Grace, a deaf setter, taught me about living life to the fullest. I've learned to embrace my passions. Although distractions may get in the way, I've found that it's best to follow my heart. I have watched the sheer delight in Grace's body as she pointed to a bird. I have felt my own joy as I finished a computer animation project or sank the winning basket in a game. Passion is the fuel for being truly happy. My friends have come in all shapes and sizes and colors. Some have had fur but most are human. They have all contributed to the person I am. Different is not something to be feared, but revered. It is not something to ridicule, but defend. My life lessons may have been silent, but I'm proud of who I have become.

Brutus

Donna Carley Tizol, Calvert County, Maryland,
Public School System

My husband and I both grew up with boxers. When it came time to decide what kind of dog we wanted to get, choosing the right breed was a no-brainer. That's when we got Lady. We had planned to breed her with hopes of keeping a male puppy for ourselves.

It was a wonderful experience for all of us to witness the birth of Lady's seven beautiful puppies. The first pup born was a big brindle male with white markings. I had to literally catch him because Lady was standing up as she was giving birth, unsure of what was really going on. This puppy, Brutus, was the one I knew we had to keep—I felt my heart in my hands at that very moment. Soon after, Lady gave birth to an all-white female pup. Well, my daughters and husband fell in love with her, too, so we decided to keep her and name her Alaska.

A few months after the pups' first birthday, Brutus had the first of many frequent epileptic seizures. He was put on phenobarbital with increasing amounts after each attack he suffered. Then one evening he had a seizure he just couldn't come out of. His body was violently thrashing about, he was losing a lot of fluids through

his salivating mouth, and his head felt so hot to the touch. Even the cold compresses we applied did nothing to aid the situation—he needed medical attention, and soon. We rushed him to the all-night animal hospital about forty miles away.

It was during that car ride that his thrashing had finally settled down, but he just laid there, totally exhausted in a semistupor kind of state while I held his paw and stroked his head. The veterinarian thought it would be best to keep him overnight and give him fluids for his dehydration. We left with heavy hearts.

The next morning, before Brutus was brought out to us, we were told terrible news: during his trauma he had run such a high fever that it had severely damaged his brain. While we weren't quite sure what this meant, we were just happy to still have him with us.

We realized how extensive the damage was once we took poor Brutus home. He didn't know how to walk. He just sat there, dazed, while Alaska and Lady wiggled their rear ends and wagged their tails with excitement at his return. We made the other dogs sit while I knelt down beside Brutus and moved his one front leg and opposite back leg, alternating sides until he got the idea of motion. My husband, while standing in front of him, gave the command "come," with every step. During one call, Alaska nudged Brutus who took two steps, then three, then four—but then he walked into the wall and stopped. We both looked at each other and knew retraining Brutus wasn't going to be an easy feat.

The next day we took Brutus to the vet. While his walk was getting more stable, we were worried because he wasn't eating or drinking enough. He also wouldn't take his medicine. The vet was also concerned and brought up the option of putting him down. Now that *wasn't* an option for us. The vet told us that Brutus would be lucky if he lived past a year after the damage that had been done to his brain. All we could do was keep trying, hoping, and praying for a full recovery. We took our dog home.

Our family was extremely patient with Brutus. I would use a bottle to squirt small amounts of water into his mouth while rubbing his neck. We'd take small pieces of moistened dog food, put them in his mouth, and rub his throat and help move his jaws around. We also continued with helping him walk indoors and outdoors. Outside it was amazing how his mother and sister would try to be of assistance and encourage him as well. Alaska would show off for her brother—tossing a toy in the air, shaking it in her mouth, and pausing just a moment to look at him and make sure she had his attention. It was as if she were saying, "Look at me! This is how you do it!" She'd drop the toy next to him, push it closer with her paws or snout, and quickly snatch it back up, trying to evoke *some* sort of emotion from him. It must've bothered Alaska that Brutus was so quiet—they used to bark at each other constantly like they were conversing with each other—but now Brutus would just sit and watch.

One day I think Brutus was either ready or simply had enough of his taunting sister, but he finally barked back. He startled all of us, especially Alaska, who jumped a full 360-degree turn in the air. Lady heard this and ran over to Brutus and started licking his ears excitedly. It was truly amazing to watch the incredible bond between our little brood.

Brutus's condition only improved from that point. Meanwhile, our friends and family told us they didn't understand why we just didn't put Brutus to sleep because of all of the medications he needed, how he had turned into a shadow of his former self, and because of all the time and energy he required. Well, he was family. After a while we were able to read him and his moods and we loved him as our own. He wasn't going anywhere. Eventually even his tail wiggle returned. We never regretted our decision for a second.

Lady and Emma

Virginia Johnson, Human Resource Coordinator;
Bill Johnson, Operating Engineer

I had two wishes in my life: to have a child and to adopt a collie. The child came first—my husband and I adopted a beautiful boy we named after him, Billy. But from the moment we adopted Billy, we realized that something was just a bit different with him. At the age of six, Billy was diagnosed with attention deficit hyperactivity disorder (ADHD). We had never heard of ADHD so we began looking for as much information on it as possible. Billy would be a child with special needs, but my husband and I both knew that lots of love and patience would help him flourish into a productive person. We were devoted to helping him succeed in life.

Was this a prelude of what was to come later in our lives? I'm not sure. But when Billy turned sixteen, I decided it was time to get that collie I always longed for. I looked around, found a reputable breeder, and found my puppy. We named her Lady and excitedly took her home.

That's when I noticed, almost instantly, that Lady's eyes did not look right. They were very small and unlike any collie's eyes I had seen before. I made an appointment to take her to the vet and in the meantime played with her and loved her anyway.

The vet told me what I was sort of thinking in the back of my mind: she couldn't see, not even a little bit. In fact, her eyes were completely detached from the rest of her. I cried for a week but then eventually got myself together and decided that with lots of training and even more patience she would be just fine. I knew what Lady's fate would be if I brought her back to the breeder— and no way was *that* going to happen.

I discussed Lady and her situation with my son and together we decided we'd dedicate as much guidance, time, and unconditional love into helping her become the great dog we knew she already was. We were both up for the challenge.

Today Lady is a therapy dog and has worked in many schools and at our local hospital. She especially does well with children with special needs. The kids look at her and think: *Hey, if she can do it, so can I!* It's amazing to watch her interact with them. Lady also wows everyone with her ability to perform on agility courses. She has even beaten out dogs that can see perfectly fine because she is so obedient.

Lady also volunteers with the Pets with Disabilities organization in our free time, helping other blind dogs find loving new owners. At one of these events, a collie rescue group approached us about Emma, a young collie that needed a home. Emma had been chained to a tree for her first six months of life and as a result, her eyes never seemed to mature. We didn't give it a second thought—Emma became part of our family right then and there. Emma, despite her bad upbringing, is now getting the care she deserves. Over time she has become a very happy girl and gets along great with Lady.

So, you see, my two life wishes came true, and then some. With the untimely recent death of our young grandchild, I've never had to rely on Lady and Emma more. I have a unique bond with my beautiful blind collies and I think that training them and caring for them brought me and the rest of my family closer together in the process as well. Blind dogs' greatest need is to have complete trust in their owners. I know mine realize I am their bridge to the seeing world. That makes our relationship very special, something I cherish and will never take for granted for as long as I live.

Samm

Michael O'Brien, Wal-Mart Distribution Center;
Kathy O'Brien, Resort Waitress

I wish we could say Samm was an angel from the get-go, but when we took him into our family to live with us as a puppy, boy—was he a terror! A full-blooded border collie, Samm was born with a disability that didn't allow his eardrums to form correctly, leaving him completely deaf. The breeder and the first family he sold Samm to were both unaware of this. The family showed concern when the rambunctious little pup wouldn't listen to their commands. Upon finding out he was deaf, they decided that a deaf dog wasn't suitable for their situation; they had a working farm and were afraid that Samm wouldn't pay attention to the machinery and he could get hurt. In the end, they sold him back to the breeder.

A little time went by and the breeder couldn't find a home for Samm, but Samm's sister, Tilly, was taken home by a friend of ours, and this friend told us about Samm's plight. At first, Kathy (my beautiful wife) and I weren't sure a deaf dog was going to be the best choice for us either. We weren't sure if we could give him the necessary treatment or care that he deserved. We also knew it would take a lot of work to train him, and we didn't know if

we would have the patience or time to do that. But we also knew that time was probably running out for Samm. We figured we had to do *something*, so we decided to take Samm home and give it our best.

Almost immediately, we found that a deaf puppy is a very unruly and sometimes spiteful little monster. Samm would constantly nip at Kathy and pee on the carpet. It was impossible to get or keep his attention and he sometimes acted like he didn't care for us getting into his business. On the rare occasion that we *did* get his attention, he never wanted to learn any sort of communication with us—and any form of obedience was definitely out of the question. We had to crate him when we went to work and at night before we went to bed. Most nights he would cry himself to sleep. The stressfulness of it all was breaking our hearts, and we started to question whether or not we had made the right decision to take Samm home with us. But we didn't want him to leave either; it wasn't fair to him to have to live his life going from one home to another. We decided to try harder to train him.

I'm painting this picture of a wild, uncontrollable puppy for a reason. We have heard other stories from friends and on the Internet about families with deaf puppies having all kinds of trouble but who do not give in. And we can attest to the fact that a deaf puppy—if trained with love, understanding, and patience—will grow into a wonderful, obedient, playful dog. So, if you are reading this and you happen to have a deaf puppy and you are questioning your choice—seriously, *don't give up!*

Once Samm realized we meant business and he understood what we were trying to say to him, something sort of clicked. Slowly we became a happy family again. Now, he no longer uses a crate for anything; he is great in the house alone. He never has any accidents indoors and he will wake us in the night with a kiss if he has to go out. He walks calmly on a leash and plays off a leash on our property. He obeys our property lines. (How? I'm not exactly sure . . . we never taught him that!) He also loves to run—border collies have a lot of energy, and he's no exception. He even has his own seatbelt harness he wears when he goes for a ride in the truck or the car. He loves to play Frisbee, and even does a little Frisbee dance (spinning around) when he catches one. Kathy has taken him to agility classes and obedience classes, where he graduated with flying colors. He's even graduated from the AKC Canine Good Citizen Program. He loves his two cat brothers, Briggs and Brownie. Samm gets to visit his sister, Tilly, often and they play together well—and rough! Sometimes he even gets to see his older half brother, Tristan.

Samm is an exceptional dog with children and with people with disabilities too; I have an older sister, Cindy, who was born with hydrocephalus, leaving her wheelchair bound and unable to talk. Samm visits her from time to time and is completely aware of her condition. He is very delicate around her and loves her very much. He knows that she too has a disability and needs special treatment.

Samm's life changed when my wife and I had our first child on September 11, 2005. Her name is Ryleigh Josephine and she was nine weeks early. She was only three pounds at birth and spent the first two months in the Intensive Care Unit for Premature Births and babies with special needs. While she was there we brought things of hers home for Samm to smell and get used to.

When she came home she had to wear an apnea monitor—all the time in the beginning, but then eventually just at night or during naps. We needed to devote a lot of attention and time to her. Samm seemed to get depressed at first, but I think he really did an awesome job understanding why we had to focus so much on her, and he gave us the time we needed. He never got jealous or spiteful of her, and he definitely sees her as a part of our pack. She is doing fine today and is starting to get around on her own. Samm really hasn't played with her yet, but I think that has to do with the fact that she doesn't play that much with him yet. The day she understands that throwing a Frisbee is one of his favorite things, she'll win over his heart and loyalty.

Taking in an unruly, deaf puppy was one of the best decisions my wife and I ever made, and we would do it again in a heartbeat. Samm is our son and we love him so much; we cannot picture our lives without him.

Buffy and Buddy

Carolyn Koch, Retired Medical Assistant;
Don Koch, Retired from General Motors Parts Division

I remember the exact day: May 13, 2004. I had been feeling real sick with flulike symptoms and no matter what I did I just couldn't seem to get any better. In fact, each day I seemed to feel worse. My husband finally convinced me to go to the emergency room. I briefly met with the ER doctor who immediately knew my condition was very serious and that the hospital wasn't equipped to help me. That feeling was nerve-racking.

The hospital immediately ordered a helicopter to fly me to Georgetown University Hospital in Washington, DC. As I was being placed on the gurney, I turned to my husband and told him how much I loved him and to please take care of my babies—my two very young cocker spaniels, Buffy and Buddy, if for some reason I didn't return home. Shortly after that I fell into a coma for nearly a week.

*   *   *

I woke up in my hospital room to two little stuffed dogs in my bed. My husband had placed them there. Even though it sounds silly,

they gave me hope and all I could think about was getting better and heading home to Buffy and Buddy. If only it was that easy. Doctors told me I had Wegener's disease, a fatal disorder in which the body's immune system attacks its own blood vessels, and in my case it was attacking my kidneys. I ended up staying in the hospital for over two months, lost both of my kidneys, and nearly lost my life—several times. Through the grace of God, the love of my husband and of my two dogs, I rebounded and was able to finally go home. I was a living miracle. To this day, I credit all of them for the reason I'm still on this earth today.

Fast-forward two years: I notice Buffy, now three years old, having a lot of trouble simply walking. I monitored her for a while, but she didn't seem to get better. I decided to take her to the vet and that's when my heart sank—Buffy had a degenerative disk disease and soon would no longer be able to use her back legs. Now it was my turn to take care of her, just as she had looked after me during my illness and recuperation period. You see, Buffy and Buddy would lie by my bed—and often *on* my bed—on my road to recovery. My husband and I had to figure out a way to allow Buffy to be mobile and independent again.

It's strange how things have a way of working themselves out. We just so happened to live right down the street from Mike and Joyce Darrell, founders of Pets with Disabilities, and decided to take a ride over to their home. We pulled into their driveway to find three of their dogs just living it up—and in wheelchairs no less! This gave us so much hope. Mike was great—he got a wheelchair fitted to Buffy and she was rolling around with the rest of 'em in no time. We were so excited to see Buffy out and about and independent again.

It may sound hokey but I truly believe I was kept alive to help Buffy. Now I have the chance to support her and give her the quality of life she deserves. She still has a lot of life left. I was told several times to put her to sleep, but there's no way I could do that—especially after knowing she had helped me through my illness and continues to help me even though she too has become disabled. She is a walking, rolling miracle for us and we appreciate her—and Buddy—every day.

Chico

Kristin Davis, Realtor; Patrick Davis, Journalist/
CNN Washington, DC

It was December 2004 and I was Christmas shopping with my mom and sister. It was late and the mall was about to close, but we just had to stop at the pet store to look at all the puppies—it was a tradition I always observed whenever I'd go shopping. That's when I met Chico.

The second I saw him I instantly knew he was going to be mine. I asked the salesperson to take him out of his cage so we could play for a little while. He seemed happy and healthy and was definitely full of energy. My mom, sister, and I looked at each other and I smiled. I went to the register to put a deposit on the little guy. I told the salesperson I'd be back the next day to pick him up.

Meanwhile, I never told my husband, Patrick, about Chico. I wanted him to be surprised when he saw him. Four months prior, we had lost our chocolate Lab, Java, to diabetes. We had just recently started talking about getting another dog to keep our ten-year-old Boston terrier, Zoe, company. Needless to say, as soon as Patrick saw Chico in my arms, he fell in love too.

We had to take Chico to the vet within forty-eight hours of purchasing him, which was the pet store's policy. Our veterinarian saw no health issues. Chico was walking fine and apparently had no other problems. Excitedly, we brought our new family member home.

Two months went by and then one day we noticed Chico was walking sort of stiffly—almost as if he were losing coordination in his hind legs. Chihuahua puppies have open fontanels, which are soft spots similar to the ones human babies have, and sometimes if they're struck in the head their fontanels can swell up with fluid, resulting in a loss of coordination. We wondered if perhaps Chico had been hit sometime before we adopted him. Again, we took him to the vet, but the vet saw no signs of trauma. To be on the safe side, we had X-rays taken and that's when we discovered

the news: Chico had a severe spinal defect, meaning one day he would become paralyzed. To top it all off, the vet told us that as he grew, his spinal cord would probably become so pinched that he might not survive.

We weren't going to give up easily. We immediately took Chico to a neurological specialist to find out if there was any surgery that could be performed to help his situation. Unfortunately, there wasn't. We were faced with a tough decision. Do we wait and see what happens? Or do we euthanize him now, because the worst is inevitable? We thought about it but couldn't bring ourselves to have little Chico put down. We loved him so much and he was healthy and happy and didn't seem to be in pain. He simply had a tough time walking and getting around on his own. To relieve him of this inconvenience, we started carrying him around wherever we went. In the meantime, our vet put him on prednisone, which he's still on today, to help the inflammation of his spine.

Vet trips became more frequent, as Chico's spine had to be monitored closely for about five months while he continued to grow. He was constantly surprising all of us as he made it through his puppy months and growth spurts. He had this constant spunk about him—a love for life—that he still exhibits today. We all saw it from the day we laid eyes on him and we were confident he'd make it through this ordeal. We weren't going to give up on him.

One day, we looked into wheelchairs for Chico, so we wouldn't have to carry him around all the time and he'd be able to move around as he wanted. We weren't sure if wheelchairs are made so small—but they are. We ordered one right away, had Chico fitted to it, and off he went. He was able to pull himself around with no problem at all. Maneuvering the little chair was simple for him. I think this was the best thing we could have done for our little guy.

Chico is now two years old. None of us expected him to live this long and most people probably wouldn't have the time and patience for a dog with Chico's disability. But he deserves to live his life to his fullest potential and we're trying to make him as happy as possible along the way. And we're happy to know we were able to help him with his lifelong disability. He has truly made our home a brighter place.

Chloe, Ellyn, and the Rest of the Gang

Ann Elizabeth Echols, President/Founder of the Chattypet Web site;
Stuart Patton Echols, Assistant Professor

Some people have one dog, some have two—we have fifteen. Of our fifteen beagles, twelve of them are rescued dogs. Adults often incredulously ask us, "How can you tell them all apart?" Children say, "Wow! They all look so different!" We tend to agree with the kids—each of our dogs is unique. We have a special relationship with all of them and vice versa. Our oldest beagle is thirteen and our youngest, we think, is about six. We guesstimate the average age of our dogs is about nine and a half years.

"The Beags," as we call them, are quite privileged in terms of how they spend their days. Our friends even refer to our home as Camp Snoopy! You see, we've tried to give them living accommodations that cater to their natural instincts. This means we installed a doggie door to the immediate fenced backyard which allows them to come and go as they please. Their doggie door is located in a passthrough—mimicking a tunnel. The passthrough goes into the tiled floor walk-out open basement that serves as a big atrium for the back. There is a bedroom off of the basement

that tends to be dark because there is only one window. Inside the bedroom there's a double-sized human bed with ramps on both sides of it, as well as a few surrounding dog kennels, so the dogs can sleep as comfortably as possible. It had always been my dream to create a dog's paradise one day—we made that happen when we got four beagles. Little did we know that doing so would spark us to adopt eleven *more*.

Each of our beagles has a special story. One was found along an interstate highway with ingrown nails and a collar that had to be surgically removed, puppy mill mothers were found abandoned with full teats and continued to carry plush toys in their mouths as if the toys were puppies until their swelling subsided, others lived

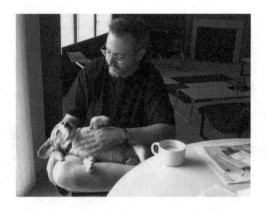

outdoors on chains, one had epilepsy and was destined to be put down within the hour, and a twelve-pound pup who had been abused has a tremendous fear of jeans and boots. Each has confided in us and released the past to find security in our forever home.

One of our rescues, in fact, came to us blind. That was Chloe. Chloe was found wandering in the woods of Pennsylvania by friends of Nittany Beagle Rescue. Over the years, Chloe's eyeballs atrophied and have since been removed. Almost immediately after her surgery, Chloe became more self-confident in her navigations—she was no longer afraid of grasses and high brush scratching her eyes. She could roam through anything, and does so happily and safely. It was Chloe who inspired my husband to seek more knowledge about disabled pets. Through this journey, he met a multitude of loving people who offered similar stories of how brave and wonderful their pets with disabilities were, and how much they had to offer.

It was on one of his "Internet visits" that he came across a small female beagle, Helen, up for adoption at Beagle Rescue of

Southern Maryland, Inc. He read Helen's biography—a touching story of another blind beagle that had a severe case of heartworms, requiring five pounds of liquid to be drained from her belly. Helen remained brave and optimistic throughout her entire treatment.

We decided to adopt Helen, but we changed her name to Ellyn. What has been remarkable about Ellyn is that she now runs and leaps through the tall grasses as if she has eyes. She hunts field mice, yodeling with her tail held high, which sparks the others to follow in her excitement. It actually *looks* like she is smiling as she leaps around. She definitely doesn't have any inhibitions about living a dog's life.

Both Ellyn and Chloe have taught us that even if one's world seems dark and without color—it's not. For color and light come through the imagination. To Ellyn and to Chloe (both of whom the veterinarians believe have been blind since birth), life's richness comes from the inside. And because of this, they inspire us daily to rekindle our spirit and strive to see beyond the present and imagine the future with joy, beauty, and love. They reach out. They aren't afraid to touch and jump. They see what we cannot through their other senses. This doesn't hold them back, but instead propels them ahead with a unique enlightenment and confidence. What a beautiful world it would be if we could all be so focused to concentrate on what we can do instead of what we can't.

Kiri

Joyce Darrell, Small Business Owner and
Cofounder of Pets with Disabilities

Cars seem to consistently play an important part in Kiri's unbelievable life journey thus far. It all started about a year ago when she was hit by one in a busy suburban area in Maryland. The accident just about took her life, but she was a strong dog and fate has a way of working its magic in strange and unusual ways.

Veterinarians didn't think that Kiri would survive, but through extensive rehabilitation and after days and days of recuperation, she slowly started to come back to life. Her tail was gone, and the damage to her nervous system had deprived her of the ability to use her hind legs, but she still had the inner drive to keep going. She was a fighter.

It was obvious that in order for Kiri to be able to function as a normal dog, she needed a wheelchair and a caretaker who understood all of her needs. Caring for Kiri became too much for her family, so they contacted my organization, Pets with Disabilities, to help find a new home for her. I got in touch with my good friends Lillie and John at Glen Highland Farm, the border collie rescue shelter in New York, thinking the best way to begin helping Kiri

was to find a family that was loyal and who appreciated border collies.

Soon enough, we found a home for her in Alberta, Canada. We wished her well, said our good-byes, and she was flown off. But her new family wasn't ready for the commitment Kiri needed, and after a few weeks she needed to be rescued once again. The only thing was she was now out of the country and very far away from help.

That's when fate stepped in. My husband, Mike, and I had planned a vacation to Montana—a camping trip with all of our pets. The night before we left, I took a quick look at the map and realized that Alberta was right above Montana. I immediately called Lillie, my friend at Glen Highland Farm, and told her about our trip. Her wheels started spinning and somehow she was able to muster up four volunteers three thousand miles away from her farm to transfer Kiri over the border and into our hands. It was some amazing work done by even more amazing people.

Soon we had Kiri and we saw that she seemed happy to see us. We understood her needs and she was smart enough to know it. When we finally introduced her to the rest of our dogs, it was clear to her that she was *home*. We bathed her and groomed her and within twenty-four hours her eyes were just as bright as they could be. We traveled back east with her to Glen Highland Farm where her new and improved wheelchair was waiting. Lillie approached me when she saw us and mentioned that she found someone who was interested in meeting Kiri—and possibly adopting her. Mike and I looked at Lillie with tears in our eyes and told her that it seemed Kiri had already found her home and she was headed back to Maryland with us.

Today Kiri races around the yard and plays with Duke, Maddie, Misty, and the rest of the gang with ease in her new wheelchair. She amazes people with her shepherding enthusiasm and even once won an award for Most Inspirational Shepherding Dog. She really is an inspiration in so many ways—and everyone who meets her definitely agrees.

Joey

Denise J. Machado, Teacher

Joey got his name because when I first laid eyes on him he was small, skinny, hairless, and helpless—much like a baby kangaroo. At first, no one thought he would survive—in fact, he was in such bad condition that no one even knew what kind of animal he was. But Joey had a few guardian angels who watched over him around the clock, and with patience, love, and understanding he soon started to recover.

Joey arrived at the humane society on November 3, wrapped up in a blanket full of blood. The shelter workers wondered if he was a cat, a dog, or perhaps a rabbit. It was hard to tell because he was incredibly emaciated, his nails were painfully overgrown, and he had horrible chemical burns all over his body. The shelter contacted me to see if I'd be interested in fostering him. My first response was "You must be joking!" I already had six dogs of my own. They told me he probably wasn't going to make it, but if he did, they needed someone to take care of him. I took a deep breath and said OK.

The first of Joey's guardian angels was a Good Samaritan who found him whimpering in the woods. Immediately, that person

took the injured dog to the local shelter. The next angel was a woman named Lauren who saw he was in need of urgent help and sent him to an emergency veterinary clinic. And then, after being called, I took over and did everything in my own power to nurture him and love him.

He fought for his life at Best Friend's Veterinary Hospital, under the supervision of Dr. Victoria Mary Hollifield, for almost a month. I went to see him several times a week, hoping that

Joey wouldn't feel lonely or abandoned. He had to be kept in an incubator—full of wounds, wrapped up in sheets, completely alone. It was heartbreaking to see him this way, but whenever I went there his eyes always met mine. I'll never forget how powerful those moments were. He really wanted to live.

At that stage, he wasn't able to walk or eat alone yet, but the amazing thing is that he still trusted people despite everything he had endured. To expedite the healing process, I decided to take him to an acupuncture expert. The acupuncturist's intense dedication to Joey made tremendous improvements in his well-being. She continues to see Joey once a week on her own time—a kind gesture. Not only has Joey gotten better physically and mentally because of these visits, he also seems to enjoy the car rides to her office.

Today Joey still has many obstacles to conquer. All of his hair follicles were destroyed as a result of the chemical burns so he'll be hairless for life. His feet pads are gone, he limps, and his little body has several scabs that will never fully heal. He still gets up two to three times each night and starts whining—possibly because of nightmares. His immune system is weak and he goes from ear infections to anemia to diarrhea all the time. His skin is extremely sensitive and it often gets very dry. In wintertime or on colder days he has to wear layers of clothing to maintain a stable body temperature.

Despite all of these things, though, he has gained thirty pounds and he seems to have a much happier outlook on life. His will to survive is so intense that he teaches me to appreciate life one day at a time. He enjoys going outside, seeing the birds, listening to different noises, and eating coconut ice cream—his favorite!

I love Joey dearly and I've become very attached to this special dog. He still has a long road to travel, with an abundance of medication, arthritis, open wounds, and infections, but whenever he looks at me as if to say, "Thanks for giving me the chance to live," that's when I know I made the right choice to take him into my life. When there is life, there is hope, and Joey is truly the personification of what it means to struggle, love no matter what, and appreciate random acts of kindness. The same way that Joey needs me, I need him to remind me of the simple pleasures in life.

Jaxx and Jesse

*Diane Frances, Business Consultant, Farmer, and
President of WorldScience; Steve Behnke, Retired from
Book Publishing Sales and Marketing*

Border collies use their eyes to direct the flock they are charged
to guide and protect. Laserlike and focused, the eyes of a
border collie are what set these dogs apart from other working
dogs. They also look deeply into the eyes of their owners, piercing
their hearts with love and affection. So imagine what it must be
like for a border collie that is blind.

Just fourteen months old, Jaxx and Jesse were two border collie
brothers living in a central Pennsylvania shelter. They had been
taken from an unsafe and unhealthy situation, and rescue workers
hoped they would be adopted soon. Unfortunately, as time went
by, Jaxx and Jesse didn't seem to get along with the other dogs
in their run. There wasn't enough space at the shelter to care for
them properly and the shelter decided the best thing to do was to
euthanize the two pups.

With the help of volunteers from Glen Highland Farm, the
border collie rescue group in Morris, New York, the two brothers
were saved and transferred there instead. There, the shelter operator discovered that Jaxx was completely blind and Jesse's sight was

very limited. She quickly realized this was probably the reason why the two dogs didn't really get along with others. Jesse, the least friendly of the two, must have been confused and startled by all the chaos around him. Out of self-defense, he would panic and attack to make the strange dogs go away. Jaxx, on the other hand, had begun to adjust so well that he managed perfectly with other dogs and with his environment, maneuvering around obstacles easily.

These brothers were so loving, so incredibly sweet, and exceptionally wonderful with people that the shelter operator knew they deserved forever homes that understood their special needs. They were both young, vital border collie mixes with *lots* of energy and interest in everything around them. They would need homes that were engaging, regardless of their disability.

Diane and Larry Frances were hoping to add a gentle dog to their family, which already included two older dogs. A special fit was needed to avoid overwhelming Bennie, their twenty-year-old Jack Russell terrier, and Mollie, their deaf, senior border collie mix. Even though Jaxx was a very young dog, when Jaxx met the couple and their dogs at their home on Christmas Eve, it was clear that he was a great fit. His gentle nature, mixed with the fact that he was carefully aware of his surroundings, helped the couple's dogs feel right at ease. Of course, when Jaxx jumped up onto the couch with Larry, it wasn't too hard to figure out he was *home*. That was a special Christmas for everyone.

One day Diane got in touch with a woman who was very experienced with caring for blind dogs over the years and who encouraged her to "talk" Jaxx through any new situation or experience. Soon, whenever Jaxx would enter a new space he would do a quick perimeter walk of the area to get his bearings and then wouldn't have another moment of difficulty thereafter.

Today Jaxx is a happy, healthy, and completely loved dog. He adjusted beautifully to his new living situation, which includes regular trips between a suburban home and a farm. Both places have invisible fences that provide Jaxx with safe and secure yards in which he can roam freely—but his favorite place is still the couch.

It took a little more time for Jesse to find his forever home. He required someone really special since he had lots of love to give but had limited compatibility with other dogs. He also needed someone to help him adapt as much as possible before all his sight was gone, a window of opportunity that would inevitably close in due time. The shelter operator was anxious to find Jesse a home as soon as possible to maximize this chance for him to still see his surroundings, even if imperfectly.

Steve Behnke heard about the border collie rescue shelter from a coworker who often volunteered there. He was eager to share his life with a special dog in need so when he heard about Jesse and his story, he set up an appointment to visit.

The first meeting won Steve's heart over instantly because Jesse, like Jaxx, was so charismatic around people. At the farm shelter, Steve was able to witness Jesse's limitations with the other dogs, but nothing deterred him from wanting to add Jesse to his life. He was ready to tackle all of Jesse's needs and the perfect match was made.

One day Steve became curious about how similar or different Jesse and Jaxx were. He began corresponding with Diane and they e-mailed back and forth, comparing notes and experiences and learning they were certainly brothers—alike in so many ways and different in others. This back-and-forth communication became key because one day Jesse experienced a seizure and Steve quickly shared the news with Diane so she could be on the lookout in case the same thing ever happened to Jaxx.

Eventually the two new dog owners thought it would be fun to hold a "family reunion" at the same location where they adopted Jesse and Jaxx. They met on Easter Sunday and the brothers curiously sniffed each other and explored their surroundings while the two owners caught up, shared more stories, and took lots of pictures.

Today Diane and Steve find comfort in knowing they're bringing a little light into their dogs' otherwise very dark worlds—the devoted dogs know their owners are their eyes to the outside world. What these playful brothers don't see is how much joy they manage to bring into Diane's and Steve's lives at the same time—or maybe they do.

Trevor

Amanda Mezick, Science Teacher

It was February 2002 and my husband, Paul, and I—OK, I—decided we should add a second dog to our home. We already had a German shepherd mix who was almost a year old (in other words, just beginning to act sane) and I figured he would be happier (and eventually calmer) with a dog playmate. After all, he spent most of his time in obedience class trying to get his classmates involved in a game of chase.

So I did a little searching on the Petfinder Web site and an unusual white female German shepherd caught my eye. When my husband and I went to meet her, we found that it was actually a German shepherd rescue. We quickly found that what was in the ad, "May have difficulty hearing" and "an older dog," actually meant, "nearly deaf" and "blind senior dog." Considering we have a large, wooded lot with an invisible fence, we thought that we wouldn't be a good match for her. Training a dog on invisible fencing requires vision and hearing.

The woman who ran the shelter was determined to send us home with a dog, so she continued to introduce us to her other residents. Our dog, Dexter, growled at every dog, that is, until Trevor was brought out. He was an emaciated, fifty-three-pound

German shepherd with floppy ears, dingy fur, lifeless eyes, and barely the energy to walk. He obediently walked on his leash, never bothering to look up at the people who were leading him. It was as if he had given up on searching for the right life and would take whatever he was given. And then they told us that he had no voice.

Someone, in a totally inhumane act, decided to have his vocal cords severed so that he could never bark. His only way of expressing his anger, joy, fear, and pain had been removed for reasons we would never know. Paul (yes, the one I dragged there in the first place) insisted that we take him home. Oddly, Dexter seemed to agree as well. And so, we wrote out our first of many checks with Trevor's name on the memo line at the bottom.

But the woman running the rescue would not let Trevor leave just yet. He was still on deworming medication and she wanted him to put on some weight before she sent him away. On our way home, we called back to tell the woman that we would definitely adopt Trevor on the condition that we could pick him up the following weekend, regardless of weight gain. Paul, a teacher, would be home from school the following week, which would give him the perfect opportunity to bond with his new pal and help him adjust to the good life. I was a wildlife rehabilitator and had worked as a vet technician. We were both up for the challenge of caring for a sickly dog.

It turned out to be a good decision. After a few days of watching Trevor drink, pant, and pace excessively, we had our vet do some blood work to find out if there was something more to his weight loss than just the obvious. Hundreds of dollars later (just the tip of the iceberg), we found out that he had a pancreatic insufficiency, which basically meant that he couldn't digest his food properly, especially fats. All that high-fat puppy chow the shelter workers had been feeding him was only making him worse. This meant that we would have to add enzymes to all of Trevor's meals for the rest of his life (a mere $130 a month) and absolutely no fatty snacks, ever.

So there we were with an adult German shepherd—probably purebred, about five years old, not neutered, no vocal cords, a pancreatic disorder, hip dysplasia, and a behavioral problem that caused him to pace and pant excessively. Like most people who adopt a dog from a rescue, we found ourselves trying to piece together his past and figure out who would do such things to a dog and what reasons the person could possibly have. When you love an animal that has been severely mistreated, it somehow makes you forever mistrust the general public. Always wondering which of these people around you would also be so cruel to a helpless animal.

Trevor, in the next year, became a sturdy ninety-three-pound dog with only one crooked ear and a perpetual smile. He romped through the woods with Dexter, ate happily, and became increasingly possessive of our home. We couldn't blame him—he finally had it all and wasn't going to let anything or anyone take it away. This posed a problem with him not having a voice, because one of a dog's first warnings is to bark or growl. After a few minor mishaps, we smartened up and put up a physical fence (did I mention checks with Trevor's name on the memo line?).

Since then we have added a border collie and a human baby to our family. Trevor is about ten or eleven and time is taking its toll on him. His sight and his hearing are both failing him, and his hips have good and bad days. He also never did get over his pacing and panting (this bothers us some days more than others). Despite all of this, we're constantly saying how lucky he is to have found us—he has had more than any dog could ever want. But we are lucky to have found him too, because the lessons he has taught us could never be replaced.

Beanie

Nancy Griffin, Church Volunteer

No one really knows where Beanie was born or where he came from but one thing's for sure: he sure is a looker! He was rescued from a parking lot by a kind person and brought to the Cimarron Valley Humane Society in Cushing, Oklahoma. With his white coat with red speckles and one unruly ear, volunteers at the humane society thought he was a red heeler mix of some sort. They decided to lovingly name him Pinky—and also realized he was deaf.

For two long years, poor Pinky watched as other dogs found new homes and he was always left behind. His spirits seemed to be dropping as each day passed and he was overlooked. One day, a woman on staff decided to take Pinky's photo and post it on the shelter's Web site with hopes that more people would be able to see him. It is because of that picture that Pinky was able to be connected with his forever family.

Nancy and her husband, Don, saw Pinky's photo online and decided to take a gamble and go check him out in person. Nancy traveled to the shelter to meet Pinky and they both made an instant connection. She decided then and there that she had to take him home.

Pinky was a bit shy and it took some getting used to when he was first introduced to Don, but after a little time, he soon found his place in both of their hearts—and on their bed. The couple decided to change Pinky's name to Beanie, which fit him better, and began loving him from the start. It took a little while for Pinky to get accustomed to his new owners and surroundings, but once he grew accustomed to everything, he began to live a dog's life for sure.

Now Beanie enjoys all the luxuries. He gets to enjoy sleeping on a big bed, walking twice a day, eating good meals, napping in the sun, traveling, and best of all, being incredibly loved. One of his favorite things to do is to ride in the church van that his human "dad" drives every Sunday morning when the boys and girls are being picked up for Sunday school. He adores all of the attention he receives from the children.

Then something happened to Beanie that he didn't like and didn't understand. As Nancy was taking him on one of his many daily walks outdoors, she noticed he was sort of dragging one of his hind legs. She took him to a veterinarian for some X-ray work and they saw there was some serious leg damage. It seemed he had been hit by a car before his shelter days and he needed to have surgery to repair the damage. Luckily, the surgery went fine and his leg is all healed now. He doesn't limp and best of all he doesn't experience pain when he walks anymore.

The shelter workers took great care of Beanie for two years and never lost hope that he would be united with a family who saw all of his potential and could see beyond the fact that he was a special needs dog. Today Beanie couldn't be happier with his new family.

Moxie

Marjorie Conn, Actress

Moxie! It's been a trademark for a popular soft drink since 1884. I remember my grandparents drinking Moxie. It also means courage, determination, energy, and pep. Moxie is a wonderful word conjuring up pleasant memories from my childhood, but that's not why I adopted my sweet, one-year-old paralyzed dog from Puerto Rico that fittingly was given the same name. It was Moxie's face that I fell in love with when I saw her picture on Petfinder.com. And she absolutely lives up to her name. She has moxie through and through.

My handsome and loyal greyhound, Frosting, died in February 2006. He was thirteen years old and we had been companions for six years. He had three homes before me. People would sometimes wonder why he had been returned to the shelter so many times, but I'd simply smile and reply, "We were waiting for each other."

My other greyhound, Irving, took to Frosting's bed after Frosting died. He lay there with such a pitiful look in his eyes. It broke my heart. Seeing Irving so depressed is what prompted me to take *just* a quick look on the Internet to see what else was available out there. And, through tears, that's when I came across Moxie's

precious little face. That quick look became a long look—and I found myself beginning the adoption process all over again.

I found out that Moxie had been run over by her owner and her back was broken, leaving her incontinent and her hind legs paralyzed. Her owner decided the best thing to do was to have Moxie euthanized. However, when the veterinarian opened her cage she somehow got away and began scooting down the hall. As if fate intervened, a saint of a woman—someone who rescues dogs—just happened to be there and refused to have Moxie put to sleep. She took Moxie home with her and posted the dog's picture on the Internet in June 2005.

Well, it was March 2006 when I saw Moxie's picture and decided I had to adopt her. Unfortunately, there was no support from my friends. They all warned me: "You don't know what you're doing!" "You're in a state of grief." "You're on the rebound." "Frosting died only two weeks ago." Truth be told, all my friends were right.

They even almost convinced me to change my mind, but something deep in my gut told me to proceed with the adoption. The adoption agency, Stray from the Heart, arranged for Moxie to be flown from Puerto Rico to New York. One of the agency workers even drove me to the airport to pick up little Moxie. The first thing Moxie did when she was released from her crate was to give me a big kiss. It certainly was love at first sight for me.

It took a couple of weeks through trial and error to figure out how to care for Moxie. For example, now I know what size of disposable baby diapers fit her best and that I can cut a little hole in them so that her tail can fit through. The adult incontinence pads are fabulous for all kinds of uses including using them as towels when I don't have access to a washing machine. I found great nylon bags that are perfect to use at night so she can sleep in bed with me without worry of accidents. And I got her a cart that she uses to help her get around better.

Irving and Moxie adore each other. They are so cute when they play together, nuzzle each other, and even chase each other around. What a delightful pair: one of the fastest running dogs

in the world and a dog on wheels! Best of all, Irving has regained his joyful demeanor. Moxie is able to do everything and go everywhere. Sometimes the three of us take really long walks by the ocean and she'll roll off to go swim in the shallow water in her cart, traipsing through seaweed and sand. Other times we all go camping in the woods and sleep in a tent.

While we're enjoying life so much right now, I still grieve for Frosting, but Moxie has helped me in the grieving process. The night after I adopted Moxie, I had an interesting dream. I was in a strange location and I couldn't find Irving or Frosting and so I became frantic. I was outside calling and calling them. Suddenly, Frosting appeared down the road and he began running toward me as fast as he could. When he got to me, he jumped up and began hugging me. I woke up and there was little Moxie, asleep in my arms.

Doyle

Jennifer Hill, Communications Coordinator at Otterbein College

Doyle has a strong hunting instinct and I take him walking in the woods so he can track with my help. He never catches anything, but he loves to try. You see, Doyle is an old, blind hound dog, but you'd never guess it by looking at him and how happy he is today.

In the fall of 2004, I adopted a senior beagle, Sherlock, from my local dog shelter in Columbus, Ohio. He had been in a cage for three months. Seeing him cling to the one volunteer who took

him home to bathe him before an adoption event showed me what a loyal dog he was—and so he came home with me that day. Two months later, I adopted a second beagle, Watson, to keep him company.

For nearly two years, my family of three cats and two dogs was complete, that is, until the day I stumbled across the Pets with

Disabilities Web site. I don't remember how I found the site, but soon I was looking at the new dogs on a weekly basis. In July 2006, I saw Humphrey, a blind, geriatric redtick coonhound-beagle mix in Bowling Green, Kentucky. His online story said he had been dumped from a car into a busy intersection. He stood there, confused and turning in circles as he tried avoiding the cars that swooshed around him, until a woman rescued him from the road and took him to a high-kill shelter. After reading this heartbreaking story, something inside told me he needed me. I knew I could provide him a good home during his golden years.

By the time I contacted the shelter listed on the Web site, a Good Samaritan had paid to have him released to a veterinarian in Bowling Green. That person also paid for major dental work, neutering for his enlarged prostate, microchipping, and to have a mass removed from his flank. I contacted this woman who conducted a background check on me and then released him to me. I drove five hours each way to and from Bowling Green to bring him home. The veterinarians in Bowling Green could not have been happier to see him going to a good home. He had touched them all deeply.

I renamed my new hound "Doyle," after Sir Arthur Conan Doyle, author of the Sherlock Holmes mysteries. At first, Doyle was reluctant to trust me, only relying on me when necessary. He walked the perimeter of the house for a few days, getting used to the layout, and Watson, one of my two other dogs, helped me teach Doyle how to take the three steps to the fenced-in yard—acting as Doyle's personal seeing-eye dog. Doyle quickly learned the commands "careful," "step up," and "step down," and impressed everyone at his new veterinarian's office with his sweet temperament, manners, and progress in settling into this different way of life.

Once Doyle became more comfortable, he began trotting in the backyard like a puppy. He even learned how to get up on the couch and bed, just like his sighted brothers. Somewhere along the way, he managed to develop a deep level of trust for me, as well as the people I introduce him to. I think my friends and family, with their incredible kindness, have given him a new opinion of people. One friend brought him a toy the week I adopted him, and my young nieces are proud to show me how gently they can pet him. He now loves people and laughter, which makes him very excited. He also loves to cuddle and knows how to get attention. He sleeps alongside his dog brothers and gets along wonderfully with my cats, even when they sneak up on him.

I often take Doyle to local dog events to spread the word about the joys of adopting a blind dog. He knows how to work the crowd and is trying to become an ambassador for blind dogs everywhere. I will always be grateful to the Pets with Disabilities organization for completing my family. Without their good work, I wouldn't have the love of my ol' blind dog.

Chester and Daisy

Dawn Hayman, Cofounder of Spring Farm CARES,
Clinton, New York

Chester and Daisy came to our facility from an animal neglect case. Beagles, estimated to be about two years old, unspayed and not neutered, they lived their lives since they were eight months old in crates, hardly ever getting out. They ate, drank, slept, and urinated and defecated in the same small crates they lived in. There were twenty-five dogs altogether that were rescued from these horrendous conditions, but Chester and Daisy came to Spring Farm CARES because of another unique situation: they were both born with five legs.

Littermates, they were more than likely born this way as a result of inbreeding. Each of these pups had a normal left front leg, but their right front legs had extra partial limbs growing off the normal legs. It rendered both of their right front legs completely useless; basically, the dogs were dragging around the extra weight of two

limbs on one. But these puppies were charmers and we were all taken aback by their incredibly loving personalities.

However, their futures seemed uncertain. Not housebroken in the least and unable to be crate trained (since that was all they really knew), we couldn't fathom what kind of homes we could find for them. On top of that, our facility was completely full and we had to put them in a kennel in our heated garage. It was the best we could do, but to them, it was a palace.

Our vets confirmed what we hoped would be the case: their double legs could be amputated. They would then be three-legged dogs, but in reality, they had only been using three legs their whole life anyway. First, we had to get them back into condition. Because they were hardly ever out of their crates, their muscles had atrophied a great deal. They could not walk far without having to lie down to catch their breath. It was hard not to get emotional watching them struggle. But eventually, after two weeks of being with us—being cared for properly and eating a good diet—they began to blossom. They were able to go into our fenced-in yard and be beagles, nose to the ground. With their improved condition, they could soon undergo the necessary surgeries they faced.

Chester was able to be neutered and have the leg amputated all in one surgery. He did splendidly. Much to our amazement, within one day after surgery, he was already walking so much better. You could see the relief written all over his face. He no longer had a useless appendage dangling from his shoulder. He healed quickly and began running and playing in no time at all.

For Daisy, we had to decide which surgery to have first. The amputation was complicated in that she had two complete sets of blood vessels that had to be sorted out, so she couldn't have the spay surgery at the same time. We had to go with spaying first, just in case there was any chance she could have gotten pregnant before she came to us. Four weeks after the surgery, she was strong enough to undergo the amputation. Again, the transformation was amazing. We all stood with tears in our eyes the day we could let them off their leashes in our dog yard for rough-and-tumble play. We were thrilled to be able to help make such a difference in their lives.

Housebreaking was our next hurdle and we had quite a struggle with that. The one thing we couldn't give them was a house to run in and homes we knew they deserved. Although they thought they had it really good we knew how much *better* they could have it. But we were beginning to think this was all beyond hope. Who would want to adopt two disabled dogs that seemed impossible to be housebroken? On top of that, we figured they would need to be adopted together because they had never been apart before. They relied on each other so much. And that's when a miracle happened.

We received a call from someone a few hours away from our farm who had seen the dogs on our Web site and instantly fell in love with them. She wanted to visit. We explained their story to her, but it didn't deter her from coming. She had another beagle that had recently lost his playmate and so she was looking for two more companions for him. She thought Chester and Daisy would be perfect.

It was love at first sight. The two dogs instantly began hugging and kissing the woman as we all stood there—beaming with emotion—knowing they finally found a real home. If those dogs thought living in the garage was heaven, they were in for a treat. Their new place had a two-acre, fenced-in yard, complete with a dog door to the house. They would be allowed on the bed at night and could sleep wherever they pleased. The woman understood the housebreaking issue and was confident that with the dog door and yard, they'd fall into a routine soon enough. We finalized the adoption and sent them home.

This story has an incredibly happy ending, but not all of them do. Chester and Daisy hit it off instantly with their new owner and beagle friend, but the woman had to put up with *months* of them peeing all over her house and tearing everything up. One day, they finally got it, and everything fell into place. With disabled pets, it takes time, love, and patience—but eventually they'll come around. It will all be worth it in the end.

Snowflake

Kim Craig, Autoworker

It was a cold January day in Ontario, Canada, and it was only fitting that our white German shepherd, Snowflake, was outside playing and just being a happy dog. She had a tendency to wander around as she pleased and she decided to go visit another dog across the street. On her way back to our house, however, she ran in front of an oncoming car—Snowflake didn't have a chance.

Her hind end was hit hard and she was thrown into a nearby ditch. Rushing to the accident site and seeing her lie there, I knew it wasn't good. She was hurt very badly and had to be rushed to the emergency veterinary clinic. The vet took X-rays and, as I expected, her hind end and pelvic area were crushed. The vet didn't think Snowflake would be able to recover from her extensive injuries and suggested that I put her down.

No way! Knowing my Snowflake and how strong a

personality she had, I decided to go with Plan B: surgery to correct the problems. Bringing her home that night, full of cuts and staples that held her wounds closed, I sat up with poor Snowflake the entire night until the clinic opened again the next day.

I brought Snowflake back and the vet warned me that she could lose the use of her right hind leg. Again, I had the choice to either put her down or try to help her get better. But she was my baby and I wasn't going to just let her go. After many more surgeries to remove splinters, it was apparent that Snowflake would definitely never fully use her right leg again. When I went home that night, I began researching wheelchairs online. I had seen them on television in the past and figured maybe I could at least find someone in my area to help. I was wrong.

However, I did find Joyce Darrell and her organization, Pets with Disabilities, after doing a Google search. I e-mailed Joyce and asked her if she knew anyone in my area who made wheelchairs for dogs. I was overwhelmed to receive a response from her that

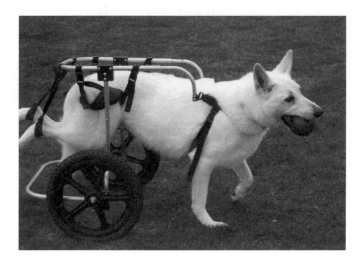

same day offering to help. She told me that her dog, Duke, was about the same size and he was about to receive a new wheelchair of his own—so I could have his old one. Words can't express how happy that made me.

As I headed to the post office to pick up the wheelchair, I became teary eyed knowing that Snowflake's freedom was sitting in a box and soon she would be on her way to playing ball and running around again. When I got there and the woman at the counter looked at me strangely, I decided to tell her what was in the package. In fact, I think I told everyone I knew—and didn't know—about the chair that day.

It only took Snowflake a week to fully figure out how to get around in the chair. From that moment on, she had her legs back. She loved going for walks again—and sometimes she'd even go for jogs with me. She had a whole new outlook on life—and so did I. I learned to appreciate the little things a little more.

During the summer of 2004 Snowflake began to get sick. To this day, I'm not exactly sure what caused her to grow ill, but the vet said that sometimes this happens to animals after traumatic accidents. Perhaps because Snowflake had to go through so many surgeries, her system was worn down. Later that fall, after two weeks of hand feeding her and after her breathing had gotten more and more difficult, I made the hardest decision of my life to help her pass on. Our vet was wonderful. He came to the house with his helpful assistants, who had also cared for her when she was in the hospital, and helped her pass on peacefully.

A little while after, I contacted Joyce and told her about my family's loss. I also asked her if we could keep the wheelchair in our area, as this type of help wasn't available in Canada and mostly unheard of. She agreed and so I posted a flyer of Snowflake's story on our vet's bulletin board, informing others of the option of a wheelchair if their pet ever became disabled. A few months after Snowflake's passing away, I received a call from our vet—he had a new candidate for the wheelchair.

After meeting the new candidate—an adorable Lab named Apollo that was also paralyzed—we were happy to know that the wheelchair would be put to good use in giving another dog his freedom again. Apollo only used the chair for a short while because he was elderly and his health eventually deteriorated, but the chair continues to get passed along from dog to dog as it's needed. Slowly but surely we are allowing family pets to move and be alive again, even if it is for a brief time.

Maddie

*Sharon A. Espinola, Corporate/Marketing Communications
and Public Relations Professional and Volunteer at the
St. Francis Society Animal Rescue, Tampa, Florida*

Seven months after finding the perfect home for Maddie in Maryland, I still keep her picture on my desk at work. My coworkers ask about her all the time. My family members often mention her with admiration in their voices. People who contributed to her care want to know how she's doing. And she continues to make a difference in the lives of those who know her.

Even though she's little, Maddie is credited with saving the lives of countless dogs rescued by the St. Francis Society Animal Rescue. Who would have thought that one tiny dog—broken in body but definitely not in spirit—would be such a miracle maker?

Maddie was hit by a car on August 6, 2004, in Ohio. Her back was broken and a vertebra was crushed, but she was still very much alive. When her family decided they no longer wanted her, she went into the care of a woman in Tampa. As the months passed, the woman's endurance and resources were stretched to the point of breaking, for in addition to Maddie, she was caring for another paralyzed dog and fostering a few cats too. By the middle of January 2005, she contacted the St. Francis Society Animal Rescue for help.

As a longtime volunteer with St. Francis Society, I think back to my e-mail exchanges with Maddie's foster mom about this energetic little girl. I learned the situation was desperate: Maddie would be euthanized if someone didn't step forward to take her in. What I didn't know then was that this would not be the first or last time Maddie's life would be on the line.

I reached out to our team of volunteers to see if someone could take Maddie immediately and help find her a forever home. When I visited Maddie's foster home to deliver diapers needed for both dogs, it was obvious to me that Maddie had *no idea* she was paralyzed. She used her front legs to get around the second-floor apartment, dragging two lifeless back legs behind her like it was nothing. The raw little toes indicated that she was active. She was happy to meet me and had something—something you can't quite put your finger on—that made her very special. Euthanasia didn't seem right for her. Her will to live was too strong. She had suffered so much and had come so far; all she wanted was to be loved and to play like any other eighteen-month-old dog.

When I got home from that first visit, I sent out another e-mail to our team of volunteers. Our new dog care coordinator, M. J. Maruca, called me later that evening and I vividly remember her saying with confidence, "How do we go about getting this little girl?"

It took M. J. and me weeks to decide what to do. Our new adoptive prospect, Joyce Darrell, lived in Maryland—it would be a long and costly trip. What if Maddie immediately sabotaged this forever home opportunity upon introducing her to her new

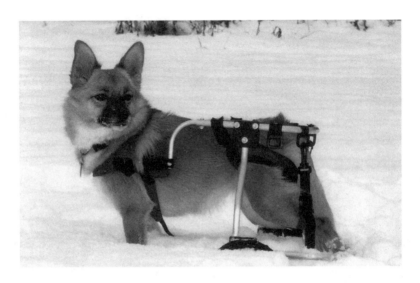

family? My husband thought we should go ahead and make the effort anyway. M. J. and I were reluctant, but we went ahead and asked Joyce to complete the adoption application. We checked her references and made plans to travel to Maryland.

With many doubts, I boarded a plane to Baltimore, with Maddie in tow, on September 10, 2005. A number of people who had followed Maddie's story helped fund the trip. It was one of the most difficult excursions I ever had to make. Carrying her through several airports, sedating her, reassuring her, changing her diaper in the Atlanta airport women's restroom, as well as going through connecting flight gates three times, had me anxious and in tears. As if affected by Maddie's outgoing nature, I found myself surrounded by kind people who genuinely cared about her story and how it would end.

Once out of the Jetway in Baltimore, I put Maddie in her cart. She walked toward the exit like the brave champ she is. Two women and a man I had met in Atlanta wanted to witness the meeting of Maddie and her new mom, so they followed me and helped me carry Maddie's belongings. One of the women recognized Joyce and her friend, Shrnique Hutchins, before I did by the WELCOME MADDIE sign they were holding. I cried at this warm reception for the little girl who had already survived so much.

We left the airport to go to Joyce's house in Chesapeake Beach, about an hour away. Maddie was still groggy and clung to me, not wanting anything to do with Joyce or Shrnique. And, when it came time for us to part ways, she even snarled at the both of them. For a moment, I thought this was going to be like the other times she was turned away. But Joyce was undaunted. She understood that Maddie had been through a lot in her short life and needed time to feel secure. Within ten days Maddie was settled in and became part of the family.

Seven months after Maddie's adoption, those of us who cared for her at St. Francis are convinced she is in the best of homes. None of us could have provided her with the home that Joyce and her husband, Mike, have provided. We're all so happy the way things worked out.

Maddie made a difference. M. J. continues to be the dog care coordinator for St. Francis Society and credits Maddie with helping her find her calling of rescuing homeless and unwanted dogs in Tampa. And, as for me, I tell this story often and have a new perspective on the life that a disabled pet can live—a very full one. I also learned a lot about the kindness, generosity, and commitment of people, not to mention faith in having my prayers answered.

Gina

Melanie Mayo, Teacher; Barbara Cohen, Homemaker;
Cathie McGrath, Homemaker

On a bright, beautiful morning in June, a young golden retriever named Gina wandered away from home. Perhaps she was chasing squirrels. Maybe she was visiting a few of her doggie friends. Either way, whatever happened between the time she left and the time Long Island Golden Retriever Rescue (LIGRR) was contacted on her behalf will always be something of a mystery. What we do know is that she was struck by a hit-and-run driver and left, paralyzed, on the side of the road.

A compassionate passerby found the dog and immediately called the local animal shelter, which in turn transported the golden to a nearby veterinary hospital. The local veterinarian conducted an exam, took X-rays, and diagnosed Gina with a number of injuries—including a spinal fracture. He knew that without specialized care, she would surely die. He contacted LIGRR and asked if the organization would assume responsibility for Gina's care if he would transport her to the local emergency center. LIGRR's answer was an immediate yes. Gina was then admitted to the emergency center for further evaluation; doctors there offered guarded hope that she could regain the use of her hind legs. Euth-

anizing this sweet pup was not an option as she had wormed her
way into the hearts of everyone she encountered.

Through all this trauma and pain, Gina remained an incredibly
sweet and loving golden retriever puppy. She gave complete trust to
everyone who cared for her. She gave kisses to hands and faces and
adored being petted. Not once through her ordeal did she show any
aggression. This was a puppy that deserved a second chance at life.

Finally the time came for Gina to undergo arduous spinal surgery and treatment for her other injuries too. Everything went
smoothly, that is, until a few weeks into rehabilitation when she
started developing complications, such as bed sores and an aggressive bladder infection. Clearly she was in need of a special foster
home that could address her medical condition.

Gina was fortunate enough to find a guardian angel to care for
her in the form of foster mom Debbie and her family. They found

that Gina was so special that they decided to formally adopt her. Today Gina's family showers her with love and also provides her with the rehabilitation she requires. Gina swims daily in a pool during good weather and uses a Jacuzzi when the cold weather sets in. The continued aqua therapy has allowed her to make some progress in the use of her hind legs.

Gina is able to move about thanks to the generosity of Doggon' Wheels, a company that donated the cart that supports her back and allows her to walk using her front legs. She is recovering amazingly well and she absolutely loves her hydrotherapy and daily massages.

No one knows if Gina will ever fully regain the use of her hind legs. But that doesn't matter—she is young and strong and she is loved, all of which work in her favor. Everyone who comes in contact with her agrees: she is a very special golden girl.

Emmy Lou

Linden Spear, Public Relations Coordinator of
The Haven-Friends for Life

Emmy Lou, a spunky little beagle, had been on the run outside our Raeford, North Carolina, facility for a while. She appeared to be an abandoned hunting dog. Every time we saw her nearby, the staff would try numerous, creative ways to lure her into our sanctuary—but to no avail. She was completely unsocialized and wanted nothing to do with us. Little did she know, the strangers trying to capture her would eventually help save her life.

One day, The Haven received a phone call from some concerned citizens who had recently seen a little beagle running loose that looked like it needed serious medical attention. We sent out our troops and immediately real-ized this was the same pup we had been trying to capture for the past few months.

From where we stood we could see that she had been shot. And believe it or not, even with a gunshot wound this stubborn beagle was still trying to run

from us. We weren't going to give up so easily this time, though, and eventually we caught her. We rushed her to the vet where X-rays were taken and the bad news was confirmed: the bullet had severed her spinal cord. That's when we were faced with a choice: we could either put her down or opt for surgery.

This dog had survived so much already that we weren't going to let a single bullet end her life. The vet told us she would never be able to use her hind legs again, but we knew she had so much spirit that she would still manage to lead a good, happy life. We couldn't give up on her and we went ahead with the surgery to remove the bullet.

We took her back to The Haven to recuperate and that's when we decided to name her Emmy Lou. We had her fitted to a wheelchair so that she could get around better and that's also when we slowly started to socialize her with humans. For a while, it seemed she had a classic case of post-traumatic stress. Loud noises sent her scurrying for cover and she was especially cautious around large men—perhaps it was a large man who shot her. Eventually,

though, she began to warm up to people and is now brave enough to go right up to anyone to say hello with her excited hound dog howls. One year later, Emmy Lou is rolling around the shelter as fast as her little cart lets her. She's our unofficial mascot that we affectionately call our Miss Social Butterfly of The Haven. She has helped The Haven in so many ways and we can't thank her enough. We proudly take her to all of our fund-raising events, to help raise awareness for all homeless dogs and dogs with disabilities. Of course, she's not a *perfect* angel—she's a menace around our cats and when we don't see her it's safe to assume she's probably up to no good. She's frequently underfoot when we conduct our vaccination days for cats and she's the first to offer to help with the world's cat overpopulation problem. You see, in Emmy Lou's mind she's still just as much of a dog as she was before she was shot.

A lot of our shelter visitors feel sorry for Emmy Lou when they meet her as she greets them at the door. (We call her our Wal-Mart greeter because she's always the first to welcome new people.) But there's nothing to feel sorry for. She's a speed racer on wheels and an extremely happy little dog. Her quality of life is excellent and she's a living life lesson: life is what you make of it. We're just happy we were there when she needed us the most.

Cheyenne

Tracie Williams, Senior Claims Auditor and Certified Dog Trainer

It was love at first sight when I laid my eyes on my new puppy, a beautiful seven-week-old German shepherd I purchased from a breeder in Ohio. Her full name was Cheyenne's Angel Eyes, but I just called her Cheyenne.

She grew quickly and was simply a gorgeous, good dog. Everyone loved her. She was so well behaved around people and other animals. I would often take her to the beach after we moved to New Jersey. She loved the ocean, always chasing the waves. She enjoyed running and fetching sticks on the soft ground and always had a good time going to the bay and digging in the sand for hours. Her life was total contentment.

When Cheyenne turned eight years old, she developed arthritis in her hip from an injury as a puppy and needed surgery to alleviate the pain. The surgery went well and she was up and about again within a week. Her pain appeared to be gone and she was running around like nothing had ever been wrong. Life was good again.

But then, about six months later, she became really bloated. I had never heard of bloat and didn't know what the signs of it were. All I knew was that something was definitely terribly wrong with my poor Cheyenne. She had always been a very obedient dog, but suddenly she was refusing to come to me when I called to her. I knew there was a problem. I called an emergency animal hospital and told the vet about her symptoms. I was told to bring her to the clinic as fast as I could.

Somehow I got to the animal hospital in half the time it normally took to drive there. The doctor brought her in immediately. After Cheyenne's exam, the doctor confirmed what the receptionist had said: Cheyenne had bloated and her stomach had twisted. She needed emergency surgery to save her life. My heart dropped when I was told she had a fifty-fifty chance of recovery. The few hours she was in surgery were the longest hours of my life. I couldn't imagine going home without her—she was my best friend.

Finally, the vet came out to tell me that Cheyenne had survived the surgery and that everything looked good and she would be fine as long as she didn't develop any infections. I was able to bring her home three days later to begin her long recovery process.

But one day on one of Cheyenne's daily walks, I noticed that one of her legs (that had been operated on six months before her stomach surgery) didn't seem to bear her weight. It would give out and she would fall. I wondered if the leg had been hurt again during the latest surgery. I called the vet and made an appointment to have it checked out.

The vet said it was possible that her leg had been hurt during the surgery because of the way the dog had to be stretched out to get to the twisted stomach. I was advised to rest Cheyenne for six weeks and give her the prescribed medications she had been taking after her surgery and bring her back for a checkup once all the medications were gone. I followed the vet's orders but, sadly, there was no improvement after six weeks. In fact, Cheyenne seemed worse.

I scheduled another appointment with the vet who examined her again and ordered X-rays that didn't show any obvious injuries. He then ordered X-rays of her spine to make sure the disks in her back weren't causing the problems. Those came back negative. So then he ordered a myelogram to determine if there were any problems with the spine or surrounding area. He said that if this test came back negative, his only diagnosis for her would be degenerative myelopathy. I prayed this wouldn't be the case..

I was at work when I got the call. I was crushed as I heard the vet tell me that she *did* have degenerative myelopathy, and I broke down in tears. I had been doing a lot of research on DM on the Internet and I knew that with this diagnosis, Cheyenne didn't have a long time to live. DM is a crippling disease that has no cure, sort of like multiple sclerosis. I tried everything on Cheyenne that I read about online: feeding her a special diet filled with vitamins and supplements, taking her to physical therapy to keep as much muscle mass as possible, treating her with acupuncture, and spending hours walking to keep her strong. Nothing seemed to slow the progress of her disease. Slowly, she began to drag her leg more. Soon it was hard for her to stand on her own and she would fall for no apparent reason. She even lost her ability to wag her tail. It was heartbreaking.

Cheyenne's physical therapist had offered to lend me a dog cart he had that would fit Cheyenne, but I was scared to death and had so many questions and concerns. How would she react to it being fitted to her? How would she relieve herself? Would she be able to move well in it? Was I being selfish for putting her in a cart? The list went on and on. I brought the cart home and reluctantly put her in it and waited for a reaction. To my amazement, she took right off in it. Within minutes she was running around the yard like she had been born with this new cart of hers. She was having fun again.

In the months that followed, Cheyenne lost all use of her back legs. But with her cart, she was still able to run and play in the yard. She was even able to continue going to the ocean. The first time I took her back to the shore, I wondered if she'd be able to navigate her cart in the sand. I had to laugh as I watched her fly across the sand in seconds—as I struggled to walk across it on my two good legs. Not only could she walk on the beach, but she could dig in the sand just as she had done when she had use of all four legs. She could even still swim in the bay. The only drawback with swimming in the cart was that she couldn't go in deep water because the cart would float up and tip over.

Eventually, DM caught up with Cheyenne's determination to live. Her speed in the cart had slowed greatly and she stumbled more during her walks. I knew the disease was spreading to her front legs. The time had come to make a decision—one I never wanted to make but knew I had to. Though her mind was bright and clear, her body was failing her. I couldn't bear to watch her struggle and fall just to walk a few feet in front of her. I contacted the vet who said he'd come to my home to euthanize her. I wanted her last moments to be at her home or on her bed, not on some cold table in a vet's office. The appointment was set.

I woke up early that morning. I took Cheyenne outside to let her walk about the yard. I brought her inside and fed her all of the things she loved to eat: prime rib with the bone and cheese. Lots of cheese. I even gave her ice cream. She had always loved ice cream, but it would sometimes upset her stomach. The vet arrived on time and gave her a shot that sent her into a deep sleep. Then he gave her a second injection that ended an eighteen-month battle with her horrible disease. She was at peace.

Two years later Cheyenne is no longer here, but her memory lives on. I couldn't save her, but I could help hundreds of other dogs. Because of Cheyenne, I joined two German shepherd rescue groups. I help with fund-raisers, donate gift baskets in her memory, and have adopted three German shepherds of my own. I'm even currently fostering a former shelter dog for one of the groups I belong to. Cheyenne taught me so much about love, determination, and adaptability that such a wonderful dog should never be forgotten.

Sweetie

Zelinda Baker, NBC Audiovisual Engineer;
Stuart Smith, Computer Support Specialist;
Joyce Darrell, Small Business Owner and
Cofounder of Pets with Disabilities

It's been said that looks can be deceiving and when you first lay eyes on Sweetie—a one-eyed, wheelchair-bound Shih Tzu that actually sort of looks like she's frowning—the first thing that may enter your mind is, Does she bite? But Sweetie's actually the biggest sweetheart you'll ever meet. And she has a charming personality to match.

At one of our local Pets with Disabilities events, I had the pleasure of meeting little Sweetie. Just twenty-five pounds, she was an adorable ball of fur—but she seemed so . . . sad. There was no life in her eyes. I learned that her owners had given her up and the sanctuary she had been staying at had recently shut down. She was now residing at a local veterinarian's office until a permanent home could be found for her. The veterinarian had brought her to the event with hopes that Sweetie would meet a potential new family. As I looked down at Sweetie, a smile crept across my face. I knew of the perfect people who may be willing to take her on.

My good friend, Zee Baker, and her partner, Stuart Smith, were passionate about rescuing small dogs. They had already had a ten-year-old fun-loving senior dog named Shawn. Ironically, Shawn just so happened to be a Shih Tzu too. As Shawn got older, he no longer was able to walk. Zee loved all of her pets and was always willing to go the extra mile for them—so purchasing a wheelchair for Shawn was nothing out of the ordinary. She wanted him to be able to enjoy the last part of his life the way a dog should. When he required more and more care as his health deteriorated, Zee never complained and gave him the best of care until the very end. I knew if she and Stuart met Sweetie, they'd fall in love with her and be willing to take on the challenges that come with adopting a disabled dog.

The more I thought about what Zee had already been through, the more I thought Sweetie would be a perfect match for her. Sweetie and Shawn even kind of *looked* similar, although dogs can never be truly replaced. And at that moment—fate can be funny sometimes—I turned and saw Zee and Stuart walking toward me and Sweetie.

Well, the rest is history. Zee and Stuart decided to foster Sweetie and soon after they decided to keep her for good. Today Stuart says that Sweetie's smile is as big as the state of Texas now that she has a great home with her new family. When she looks at them—even though she has one eye—it's obvious she's beaming with pride. She was even selected to model for their local animal shelter's 2007 calendar. Seeing her happy makes them happy, and bringing animals together with people who will love them unconditionally is what makes me absolutely enjoy the work that I do.

Marble

Lori Barrett, Stay-at-Home Mom

Marble, a Shih Tzu-poodle mix, led a normal life when she was growing up. She was purchased from a pet store by a nice, married couple with a young daughter, and she lived with them, healthy and happy, for about three years. That's when Marble's life got turned upside down.

In May 2002, she was diagnosed with thoracolumbar and lumbar intervertebral disk disease. In other words, she had a compressed disk and calcified disks and needed to have surgery, a procedure called a laminectomy, as soon as possible. Previous studies had indicated that 80 to 95 percent of dogs with disk disease tend to recover, and physical therapy is usually recommended to speed up the healing process. Marble had the surgery a few days after being diagnosed with the disease and it went well, however, she was never able to walk again on her own.

Seven months later, I had the pleasure of meeting Marble at the Cozy Inn Pet Resort in Pittsburg, Pennsylvania. I started working as a pet technician earlier that July. This special facility not only offers boarding for vacationers but also has an in-ground pool and a whirlpool for recreation and hydrotherapy. Marble was there for rehabilitation. And while she was very brave and determined to fully recover, unfortunately too much time had elapsed since her surgery, and the muscles in her back legs had atrophied. Marble was a trooper, though, and made the most of what she had. She would scoot around on her rear end while using her front legs and actually managed to do this fairly quickly. I fell in love with her during her stay at Cozy Inn.

I thought of the little dog often but never heard from her family, that is, until about six months later when they called the resort asking if anyone would be interested in giving Marble a home. She still couldn't walk and didn't have control of her bowel movements or bladder, which meant she needed diapers. The family now had a toddler at home so Marble was getting to be too much for them to take care of. I already loved Marble and understood how much care she'd require. After going home and discussing the situation with my husband, we agreed to adopt her ourselves.

We happily adopted Marble and took her home. I couldn't wait for her to meet her new brothers and sisters: Spencer, a German shepherd mix; Millie, a Rottweiler mix; four cats—Mack, Rascal, Annie, and Kierstin—and Hopkins, the rabbit. At first Marble was a little shy around her new playmates, and even growled at Spencer and Millie, but soon they learned to be gentle with her and to not get in her space.

The next day my husband found a cart on the Internet from K-9 Carts. We received it within a week. The moment we put her in it and she realized she could walk again she was elated. It was obvious she was so happy and proud of herself. She even figured

out how to make turns around corners and how to back up. I knew this cart was going to make her life so much easier and give her more confidence.

Since Marble has been using her cart, she's been very busy. She won a trophy over the summer in a walkathon for an animal shelter and was voted Most Unique Walker. She was dressed as a hula dancer, complete with a grass skirt. She also went to my church and was blessed by our priest. She was the most well-behaved dog there, I must say. And on Halloween, she sported a skunk costume. Everyone seemed to enjoy that one, especially her.

Since adopting Marble, our family has expanded yet again with the adoption of another cat, Murphy, and a lovable seventeen-year-old basset mix named Babe. I'm confident that Marble will live a long and happy life with us and the rest of our menagerie. And I'm so thankful for her K-9 cart. It really enables her to walk with the big dogs.

Roxy

Sarah Strain, High School Dance Teacher

September 25 was just another sunny Sunday. Little did I realize that a little black-and-white pup rescued from Hurricane Katrina was about to become a member of our family.

Abby Bell-Mills, and her husband, Matt, are wonderful volunteers from the Calvert County Humane Society in Maryland who rented an RV and trailer and drove down to one of the areas in Mississippi that was ravaged by Hurricane Katrina. Their twenty-eight-hour return trip ended in a field in southern Maryland. A group of volunteers, including myself, would provide assistance walking the animals through the veterinary triage areas. Tears came to my eyes as the gate of the trailer opened. Twenty-five pairs of scared eyes were staring back at us.

My heart broke for the families who had lost their pets in the aftermath of Katrina, but I knew that what we were doing was the next best thing. Initially I was assigned to a large, friendly black Lab. Sometime during the course of the day I was reassigned to a black-and-white, two-month-old pit bull mix. I held her for hours before she was finally vetted and ready to meet her foster family.

Fortunately for us, her foster family never showed up. Of course, I did the only thing I could do and took her home.

Roxy fit into our multianimal household immediately. She latched onto our older Lab, Abby, and mingled well with the two cats. In fact, I don't think she was aware that they were another species that she would otherwise naturally chase.

Roxy's arrival couldn't have been timelier. Weeks earlier, we received the horrifying news that our nineteen-year-old daughter, Lindsay, had melanoma. Surgeries and a year of treatments were imminent and our family needed something positive to focus on. Roxy fit the bill. She bonded with all of us and especially with Lindsay. Roxy spent many hours stretched out on the bed or couch next to Lindsay as she recuperated from surgeries or had to endure her interferon treatments. Her presence was very comforting and her antics kept us laughing.

Months later, we got our chance to repay Roxy for her affections. We noticed that she was standing with her hind legs together and she was becoming less active. She was obviously in pain. X-rays revealed that she never developed hip sockets. Surgery was necessary and the initial cost estimates were staggering. As a family, we agreed that we needed to research all options and find a way to save this pup who had given us so much.

Ultimately we decided on a Femoral Head Ostomy, or FHO— the surgical removal of the ball portion from both of the hip joints. The procedure would reduce her discomfort and she could still retain her mobility. We scheduled the surgery for the last week of

March 2006 and prepared ourselves to receive her postsurgery and help her begin rehabilitation.

Roxy came through the surgery beautifully and her wonderful disposition continued to shine through despite her obvious initial discomfort. She was definitely a favorite with the employees at the hospital. More important though, her prognosis looked good. We know that Roxy will never be an agility dog and she'll always have some degree of instability in her hindquarters but the one thing that will be a constant is her unwavering love and affection that came at a time when we needed it most.

Sparky

Louise F. Johnson, Retired Teacher of the Blind and Visually Impaired

Not many people can say this, but I had a happy accident. And it came in the form of Sparky, my wonderful, blind collie that I wouldn't trade for anything in the world. One day, for lack of anything to do, I went surfing (on the 'net, that is) just for the heck of it. Fun led me to "collie rescue groups." The very first dog shown on the very first group was a young, blind collie. Now, I was in no way looking to add another dog to our household as my family already had two collies. But, for lack of better phrasing, something about this particular collie caught my eye.

I thought that training a blind dog would be interesting and challenging. I had been a teacher for the blind for many years and was always amazed at what could be accomplished in spite of blindness. I decided then and there that I *had* to have that dog. I filled out the application, was accepted, and set up a meeting to be introduced to Sparky and so that he could meet my two collies as well. Everyone got along just fine from the start so the deal was sealed. Sparky was ours.

I learned beforehand that Sparky had been born blind, which probably made a big difference in his training as he had never known sight. To compensate for his lack of vision, he makes excellent use of his sense of hearing and smell.

When we arrived home that first day, he immediately investigated the whole house and quickly learned his way around. The biggest problem was that he had never been up or down a flight of stairs. He soon learned to go up but coming down was a real challenge. (Imagine not being able to see and standing at the top of the stairs near the edge of what must seem like a big hole.) We would have the other two dogs go down the stairs and come back up hoping Sparky would realize that it really was quite safe and he wouldn't just disappear. Finally, with me in front of him so he could lean on me and my husband behind him, we moved him—one foot at a time—down the stairs. He was very frightened and reluctant, but once he was down he was fine. We practiced this up-and-down method for days.

Formal training began right away at a nearby dog training school. The instructors were amazed at how independent he was and sometimes I even had to tell people that he couldn't see. We went through all the levels of training, basic through super advanced, and graduated with him passing the AKC Canine Good Citizen test.

I still wanted to continue with Sparky's training after he graduated, though, and the school had recently started instruction in Rally Obedience. I asked the instructor if she would let Sparky participate. She was quite willing so we began the Association of Pet Dog Trainers (APDT) Rally-O courses. At the time, I had no thought of competing with him. APDT allows and encourages dogs and people with disabilities to compete. Sparky did so well that we decided to give it a try. We entered trials and got a Level One title.

Today Sparky also has the distinction of being the first disabled dog to earn an APDT Rally-O title. (I beam with pride every time I think of it.) We went on to Level Two, which is done off lead, and earned a Level Two title as well—with a first place! The only real modification to the Level Two course was the jump. We all agreed that it would be very dangerous for a blind dog to be sent over a jump so we were allowed to walk up to it and he would step over. He follows my voice commands, hand clapping, and my scent.

Sparky understands many words but "come" does not seem to be one of them. If I want him to come in all I have to do is say "dinner" or "cookie" and he is in like a flash. A loud "careful" lets him know that there is danger and he will stop and wait for me to rescue him.

Now Sparky is almost six years old and about a year ago he began having seizures. We decided to suspend competitions until we had the seizures under control. He is doing well on medication and hopefully we can resume competing soon. I have learned so much about courage and determination from Sparky. I am privileged to be his "person."

Every dog deserves a chance to live up to its full potential. Both Sparky "The Ambassador" (we call him this with hopes that he and his accomplishments will be an inspiration to others) and I hope that anyone adopting a dog from a shelter or rescue organization will not pass by a dog just because of a disability. Finding ways to train your dog effectively is not only challenging, but fun as well. And having fun with your dog is what it's all about.

Nick

Jessica "Jessy" Letourneau, Battling Multiple Sclerosis;
Lance Tavares, Sheet Metal Draftsman

My boyfriend, Lance, and I were just taking a routine trip to the pet store to buy cat food. When we pulled into the parking lot, we noticed about a dozen animals outside the building. We casually commented on how beautiful this one particular dog was, sitting there looking so regal, and we proceeded inside.

When we went to pay for our cat food, I asked the person at the register if there was a rabies clinic going on outside. She replied, "No, it's an adoption clinic. Are you interested?" I smiled politely and told her I already had three cats and that I didn't need any more animals.

Upon leaving, my curiosity got the best of me anyway and I told my boyfriend I wanted to check out the cats. (Can you tell I'm a cat person?) The lady in charge of the adoptions approached us with the dog we had commented on earlier and asked if we were interested in getting a kitten. I told her we were just looking but that she had the most beautiful dog I had ever seen. She told me that he was actually there for adoption. She then started telling me about his sad story: he had been found on a median strip in the middle of a highway. He was grossly underweight, frightfully dirty, and had severe heartworm. To top it all off, he appeared to have been badly abused as well. She mentioned that whoever adopted him would have to realize he would understandably have trust issues at first.

Before I knew it, an hour had passed and we were still standing outside the pet shop. The whole time that beautiful dog sat calmly at my side. I guess it was meant to be. As I kept looking down at him and he kept looking up at me with his big, gentle brown eyes I fell in love—we decided to take him home as a birthday present for me. When we took Nick home, he was about three or four years old and still twenty pounds underweight. He was also still taking (his last) heartworm treatment. Lance and I knew we had a lot of work cut out for us, but we were willing to do it.

Even though Nick was such a pleasant dog, it seemed like life was constantly throwing him curveballs. The women at the adoption clinic said they'd usually put a dog down if it was in Nick's condition, but Nick was an exception because he was so sweet. They all took money out of their own pockets to pay for his treatment. A year and a half after we adopted him, Nick developed two tumors that turned out to be cancer. We decided to have them surgically removed and the vet was confident she got all of the cancer out. Three years after that, however, the cancer came back and poor Nick had to have surgery again. After going through all the presurgery testing that Nick was growing accustomed to, the vets found that he had an enlarged heart because of the heartworms. They had to change the anesthesia they had been planning to use so that his heart wouldn't be affected. But as soon as the sedating began to take effect, Nick had a heart attack. Fortunately for Nick (and for me), surgery hadn't begun yet and he was able to be saved once again.

After all of that chaos, I was told that Nick could never be sedated again. This meant that the vets couldn't take the cancerous tumor out. My family, friends, and I all prayed that he would be OK. Three weeks later, the vet called. She said that Nick was such a well-behaved dog that she would attempt to do a local anesthetic to remove the tumor, although she had never done it on a dog before. I agreed to the procedure, and luckily it was a great success. Nick was the talk of the hospital. Everything was fine, *finally*, or so I thought.

Shortly after that surgery Nick began having trouble getting up and walking with his hind legs. I decided to purchase a doggie wheelchair from Dewey's Wheelchairs for Dogs. I discussed this with my vet and she thought it was a good idea. Then I took Nick to a neurologist. The neurologist told me that Nick could have a

ruptured disk, or worse, degenerative myelopathy. He couldn't be absolutely sure without an MRI, which he couldn't do without putting Nick to sleep. Four weeks later, Nick was totally paralyzed from the waist down.

I know how stressful it must've been for Nick as these bad things continued to happen to him because I am only thirty-nine years old and have been fighting multiple sclerosis for sixteen years. I walk with a cane and occasionally use a wheelchair. Because of this, I have a difficult time trying to handle a one-hundred-pound Lab-husky mix that weighs only twenty pounds less than I do. He had been paralyzed for four weeks and I was beside myself. Lance and I were faced with the decision to put him down. After everything Nick had been through, this *couldn't* be the way it was supposed to end. He had so much life and love in his eyes that I couldn't bring myself to do it. Even though everyone said it would be the best thing to do, I was determined to find a way to make it all work out.

I talked with Nick's vet again and she suggested I go to an acupuncturist for dogs. Everyone around me thought I was crazy—that I would just be wasting my money and my heart would be broken in the end. Luckily, my vet refused to be defeated after all she had done and she graciously referred me to a remarkable acupuncturist. The results were astounding: after three treatments Nick was standing on his own. After five treatments he was getting up on his own and after six he was able to take steps around the house. Now Nick has celebrity status at the acupuncturist's office—they all know who he is. He only uses his wheelchair now when he goes for walks outdoors with me. We must be quite a sight: Nick with his wheels and me with my cane walking together!

I look at Nick's beautiful face and realize he would not have been here with me for the last two years if I had given up on him. He gives me another reason to wake up in the morning and go on. We both have a strong will to survive and I know there is nothing we can't get through together. Nick is incredibly happy now, especially when he chases the wild rabbits in our yard. He's my inspiration. He's my friend. He truly is my miracle.

Sara

Barbara Kerkhoff, Retired;
John Kerkhoff, Accident Reconstructionist Engineer

When Stevie Nicks of Fleetwood Mac wrote "Sara" more than twenty-five years ago, she never could have foreseen the saga of a white German Shepherd named Sara Poet of the Heart as it played out in Ventura County, California, in February and March of 2005.

Sara was the helper dog of a disabled Gulf War veteran who became separated from her owner while they were visiting Oxnard. For almost three weeks, Sara was frightened and running loose in the fields and streets of south Oxnard. Volunteers searched everywhere for her. Early one morning Sara was hit by a car in a hit-and-run accident. Her injuries were traumatic: shattered pelvis, fractured spine, and broken hind legs. The veterinarians caring for her determined she would never be able to use her hind legs again, but because of her age and sunny disposition they felt she was a good candidate for a dog wheelchair after she had an extended time period to recover and heal from her injuries.

Their predictions proved true. Sara took to her new cart as a duck takes to water. Unfortunately, though, she wasn't able to be returned to her original owner because she was now in the same

position he was in—paralyzed from the waist down—and he could no longer care for her the way she now needed to be cared for.

Sara's plight captured the minds and hearts of many Ventura County residents, as well as the print and television media and ani-

mal rescue groups throughout the country. Funds were raised for the costs of her healing and to find Sara a good home. Despite all that she had gone through—from getting lost and being on her own for three weeks to getting hit by a car and having to endure extensive surgery—she was always trusting and loving and had a definite spirit and will to survive. Her doctors and caretakers at the animal hospital fell in love with her.

The roles of life had been switched. Sara went from supporting and taking care of someone who was physically challenged to being physically challenged herself. She needed someone who was willing to put in the extra effort of taking care of her now. And as miracles tend to occur unexpectedly, one loving couple came forward. Today Sara is happily living in Helena, Montana, with her new mom and dad, Dick and Barbara Poepping. There she is the queen of the house—and of the yard. She has made friends with the rabbits and squirrels outside (although the squirrels are inclined to tease her, running up and down trees and jumping onto telephone pole wires when she barks and tries to get closer to them). She's so active to the point where she is now on her second cart. Her cart maker said he has never quite come across a dog like Sara. She doesn't acknowledge the fact that she's in a wheelchair at all.

Sara, with the help of her dad, has become an inspiration to the children in the special education classes at Fremont Junior High School in Oxnard. The children became concerned when Sara was running free, and their teacher who was helping with the rescue efforts, always kept them abreast of the latest developments. Dick and Barbara thought it would be nice to let the children know that Sara was thinking of them, and so she frequently plays pen pal with the students throughout the school year. She even sent graduating seniors congratulation cards last year and is planning to do the same in the summer.

Tag

Diane Boss, Senior Medical Technologist

Tag was full of pent-up energy and attitude, and he wasn't afraid of anything. And he was on death row in Canada. But that's when Aussie Rescue and Placement Helpline, Inc. caught wind of the deaf Australian shepherd and stepped in and took him into foster care. It's also when the most wonderful dog I have ever met came into my life.

After being rescued from nearly being euthanized, Tag came home to live in Hanover, New Hampshire, to begin his happy life with three cats, a seven-year-old Irish setter (also a rescued dog), and myself. Very quickly I found out that he had a mind of his own because no one had ever taken the time to work with him. He had no clue what "yes" and "no" meant, he couldn't respond to hand signals, and he didn't know proper behavior in a house or how to walk on a leash. He didn't know what a reward was or why rewards were given for good behavior. In fact, he didn't know the difference between good and bad behavior. With Tag, there were no boundaries. That's when I realized how tremendous a job caring for a young, deaf dog was going to be.

Our first disagreement over who was in charge occurred on the third day after I brought him home. He decided to jump onto

the kitchen counter to chase one of the cats. I grabbed him by the collar to get his attention since eye contact was out of the question. That's when he tried to bite me. *That* kind of behavior was not going to be tolerated and so I immediately held him still, all the while maintaining a dominant body position until he calmed down. It seemed to work.

Two weeks later, he tested me again. This time he backed down almost immediately. He finally recognized that I was the alpha dog in this house and at that moment, his attitude took a total about-face. He no longer needed to be in control and he began to relax and just be a dog that enjoyed his new home. We were now able to begin to explore our relationship together and how to communicate with each other. Our journey had begun.

In working with a deaf dog, it's crucial to get him to focus his attention on you. To do this, I would have to "tag" him, or touch him, in order to teach him to look at me since visual distractions can be more interesting than treats. Thus, he became known as Tag. I soon discovered Tag was a very smart dog—happy and full of life. He had a sparkle in his eyes that was totally captivating. He could have been a fear biter, being afraid of everyone and everything, but in actuality, Tag was just the opposite. He loved to meet new people, always wagging his tail and offering to be petted.

Tag loved to learn. Some owners of deaf dogs use American Sign Language (ASL) for their hand signals. Since I didn't know ASL, I used signs that were easy for me to learn and teach to Tag. If he got confused, it was usually because I didn't present the meaning of the sign clearly enough to him. When he did understand a sign, there was no mistaking the joy he felt. The hardest sign to teach him was to be quiet. Aussies love to bark (even deaf ones) and he would get so excited that sometimes I had to resort to using a squirt gun with water to disrupt his barking. He would then focus his attention on me and I would give him the sign for "quiet." If he stopped barking, he got a treat. It took a while, but eventually he got it down.

Even though Tag was deaf, being an Australian shepherd meant that he still required a lot of exercise. Although I have a large fenced-in yard, it didn't seem to be large enough for him. Remembering that cars are the bane of every deaf dog, I wanted a safe place to work with him where he could be unleashed at times. I saw a demonstration on dog agility and thought what a wonderful way for Tag and myself to learn how to do something together and have fun at the same time. On an agility course, a dog must be able to negotiate various obstacles, such as open and closed tunnels, an elevated walkover, an A-frame, seesaws, weave poles, a pause table, and several types of jumps while taking directions from its handler. But how do I begin to teach a deaf dog the complexities of an obstacle course? Unfortunately for me, there were no dog agility instructors in my area who had ever worked with a dog like Tag.

That's when I met this wonderful instructor who was also a dog behaviorist and U.S. Dog Agility Association (USDAA) trial judge, Sharon Wirant. Sharon had never worked with a deaf dog before, but she was willing to learn along with Tag and me. We started to teach Tag to respond to various hand signals that would tell him what I wanted him to do on the course. Sharon also taught me how to be consistent with my timing and the use of body language for giving directions. Immediately, this sport clicked with Tag. He looked at me to see where I was and to receive the next hand signal as we made our way around the course. He responded with enthusiasm and could combine learning with running, jumping, and climbing. To him, life couldn't get any better. Tag and I were becoming partners in the truest sense; we were now a team.

We began competing in Canine Performance Events (CPE) and USDAA agility trials where we have been quite successful in our performance. People who know Tag are thrilled to watch him compete in the ring. Often conversations outside the ring would pause so they could watch him perform on the course. Audience members have told me that to see a disabled dog compete at Tag's level is awe inspiring. They are amazed that his performance often exceeds that of a hearing dog. But for me, Tag is just Tag. The bond that has grown between us is what makes him successful. I know someday we will qualify for our own agility championship.

Tag has become such an incredible dog since those early days so long ago. The bond we have together is very special. Tag is very much like an extension of myself. He is my constant companion and friend—the joy of my life. The happiness he projects in his life is apparent to all who have met him. He is an exceptional dog who just so happens to be deaf.

Sweet Pea

Volunteers and Staff of the American Society for the
Prevention of Cruelty to Animals Volunteer

Sweet Pea's incredible story actually began in 1866 when New York shipping heir Henry Bergh, fed up with the animal abuse that he witnessed daily on the streets of New York City, decided to single-handedly do something about it. In the entrepreneurial spirit of the era, Henry founded America's first humane organization and named it the American Society for the Prevention of Cruelty to Animals (ASPCA). But that wasn't all. In just nine days he also persuaded the New York State Legislature to pass laws making animal abuse a criminal offense and to give the ASPCA the power to enforce these laws. Today, one of Henry Bergh's greatest legacies is that New York City has one of the finest, most experienced humane law enforcement departments in the country.

Fast-forward to September 2005. Employees at Animal Care and Control, New York City's public shelter, saw a case that would make anyone's blood boil. A four-year-old tan and white female pit bull—filthy, emaciated, and with paralyzed hind legs—was picked up in Brooklyn. Upon examination by a veterinarian, the ASPCA's Humane Law Enforcement department was called.

After reviewing the vet's findings, ASPCA officers concluded that Sweet Pea, the name given to the poor pooch, was a victim of animal abuse. She was immediately transported to the ASPCA's Bergh Memorial Animal Hospital for treatment. Sweet Pea's owner was arrested for animal cruelty shortly after and signed over his rights to the dog to the ASPCA.

The cause of Sweet Pea's paralysis—whether deliberate, accidental, or the result of an infectious disease—remains a mystery. Although she quickly gained weight and is an avid eater to this day, her health has always been fragile. She is prone to urinary tract infections and needs anti-inflammatory medicine daily to keep her comfortable. She is only partially continent too. Even after her rescue, Sweet Pea suffered from kennel cough, giardiasis, and ringworm—which was particularly trying because it limited her contact with her devoted caretakers, whose touch she craved.

But Sweet Pea's story isn't all hardship. She soon gained strength to rapidly scoot around on her front legs and exploit any opportunity to make speedy, unscheduled—and often comical— exits from her kennel. Rebounding from her rough past, nothing dimmed her intelligence or desire to get her way. She quickly realized, for example, that two human hands are better than one. If someone strokes her with only one hand, she pokes at the other with her soft muzzle. Sweet Pea thrives on human contact so much that she even enjoys having her teeth brushed.

But Sweet Pea isn't a total pushover. Rather, this once sad, crippled dog retains the feisty character of her breed and in no uncertain terms will vocalize her disapproval of unfamiliar dogs in a strong voice that has not been dimmed by her disability. With the pets and people she's attached to, she is a loyal and affectionate canine.

Sweet Pea's progress reached new heights when ASPCA volunteer Esther Koslow contacted Eddie and Leslie Grinnell, owners of Eddie's Wheels, a manufacturer of carts for disabled dogs based in Shelburne Falls, Massachusetts. The Grinnells built Sweet Pea a customized two-wheel cart, giving her newfound mobility. Trundling along, Sweet Pea often attracts the attention of curious children. Her positive attitude demonstrates that a disadvantage need not be debilitating. In fact, Sweet Pea and another dog, Baby (also outfitted with an Eddie's Wheel cart), are famous for engaging in cart races, and Sweet Pea often flips her own cart over to enjoy a roll in the grass.

The ASPCA made Sweet Pea available for adoption in October 2005. Even after the headway made since her rescue, placing her in a permanent home remained a challenge. No matter how

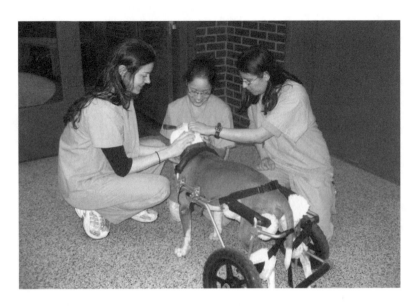

loving the staff and volunteers are at a shelter, no animal should have to spend the rest of its life at one. Sweet Pea needed a special adopter, one with experience who could enable a handicapped dog to fulfill its potential. Sweet Pea's story was featured in several media outlets, but still there were no takers. Then, in June 2006, Eddie and Leslie agreed to foster Sweet Pea for two weeks. Only twenty-four hours after she arrived, the Grinnells decided to adopt her. Sweet Pea's new family now includes a disabled dachshund named Daisy, a Doberman named Autumn, and a Rottweiler-Doberman mix named Toby.

Today Sweet Pea continues to live up to her name. Each day she becomes more trusting and more curious. Recently she found her way upstairs, around the building and inside the reception area, so she could lie down under her new mom's desk. She loves her new family and they adore her.

Hardship often beckons compassion, and to that extent, Sweet Pea's story is a shining example of the humane community Henry Bergh envisioned when he founded the ASPCA over one hundred years ago. We still have a long way to go, but slowly and surely pets and animals are finally getting to lead the better lives they all deserve to live.

What to Expect When
Living with a Deaf Dog

Lori Skinner, Caretaker of a Deaf Dog

Living with a deaf dog has all the joys, worries, and frustrations that come with living with a hearing dog. However, deaf dogs are a dog first, their breed comes second, and being deaf is third. If the dog is a puppy, then the trials of puppyhood will be thrown into the mix. Deaf dogs have individual personalities just as any dog, influenced by breed type and early socialization experiences. The keys to raising a deaf dog are openness to a new experience, willingness to learn a new language, and a commitment to consistency. The great thing about dogs in general is their ability to adapt and go with the flow.

When it comes to using hand signals to communicate with the deaf dog, there are no right or wrong signs. It's more a matter of using the same sign consistently each time. As with all dogs, positive training is the most effective. One must never use the hand as a weapon for punishment.

Numerous tricks of the trade can be used when living with a deaf dog. To get a deaf dog's attention, you can stomp your foot on the floor or flick a light off and on. There are also electronic collars available with a vibrating feature that can be used to call a dog. It is recommended to crate train deaf dogs, which gives them a safe space to feel comfortable in. Some deaf dogs prefer an open-style crate, while others prefer a more closed-style—sometimes completely covered.

Training classes are recommended for *all* dogs, including deaf dogs. It is not necessary to find a deaf dog trainer. Many positive trainers are willing to work with deaf dogs, but it is always wise to ask before signing up. Most deaf dogs respond well to a lure-and-reward style of training. Deaf dogs can be clicker trained just like hearing dogs. Instead of a sound click, you can use a small flashlight or a simple thumbs-up sign. Avoid using a laser light, which could possibly damage the dog's eyes.

Unless your deaf dog has very reliable recall, it is wise to keep it on a leash when outside. If you have access to a fenced area, your dog will greatly appreciate the opportunity to run free. If there are no fenced areas, a long lead can give your deaf dog a chance to run, play, and explore. It is important that your deaf dog has a collar, home information tag, and/or is microchipped in case it gets lost. Many owners include a tag on their dogs' collars that indicate they are deaf.

It is a common myth that deaf dogs will startle easily and bite. To condition your deaf dog to being awakened, tap him on the shoulder and offer a delicious treat numerous times throughout the day.

A deaf dog's health is comparable to that of its hearing counterparts, with certain problems known to affect specific breeds. The only behavioral problem that may be seen more in deaf dogs is the tendency to chase shadows or lights. While this may be a charming outlet for activity, it can quickly become an obsession. For this reason, it is recommended that you interrupt the behavior and redirect the dog to something more appropriate.

Although deaf dogs are prohibited from competing in AKC events, many participate in competitions such as agility and obedience in other venues. Deaf dogs can make wonderful therapy dogs and have even been used in search-and-rescue operations. However, many deaf dogs are never given these opportunities because they are euthanized by their breeders once it is apparent the dogs are deaf.

What to Expect When
Living with a Paralyzed Dog

Joyce Darrell, Small Business Owner and
Cofounder of Pets with Disabilities

Dogs can lose the use of their back legs for several reasons: old age, accidents, or birth defects. In the past, this disability was pretty much a death sentence for the dog. But in recent years, wheelchair technology for dogs has improved tremendously. The wheelchairs are lightweight with all-terrain wheels and a harness system that is human friendly.

The most common question people ask me is: how do the dogs cope with being in a wheelchair? My answer to them is that most dogs adapt to them beautifully. The humans are the ones who need to be able to cope with this new lifestyle change more than the dogs. As with all dogs with disabilities, it takes a lot of human patience. Having a dog in a wheelchair is a big decision for many people. They become worried about their dogs' quality of life and, of course, their own quality of life too. Many folks feel that some-one needs to be home twenty-four hours a day, seven days a week with their dog, depending on the severity of the paralysis. The truth is, most dogs will do fine for several hours on their own.

They basically will sleep while the caretaker is at work. Just like able-bodied dogs.

There are many factors to think about before you decide whether to get your dog a wheelchair:

1. Most important, the dog's two front legs *have* to be strong.
2. Does your dog have a good appetite and good digestion?
3. Does your dog have the will to get up and go?
4. How heavy is your dog? The weight of your dog can be a serious issue. You will encounter times when you will need to *physically pick up* your dog so that he does not drag and hurt himself. Dogs will be dogs, and they will drag themselves to get where they want to be. You have to think for them.
5. Will your schedule allow you to take time out to place your dog in the wheelchair and go out for daily activity? This is physically and mentally important for the dog. Whether playing with a tennis ball, catching a hurled Frisbee, trail walking, or just putting their nose to the ground and smelling the earth, remember, *they are still dogs first.* They will attempt to do all the things an able-bodied dog will do. If they physically can't, they will figure out how to do it. For example, our dog Duke was surrounded by a bunch of dogs at dog camp this past year. They were all leaping into the river. Duke *knew* he was unable to leap like the other dogs, so he figured out how to join them a different way. He slowly navigated himself down into the river with the other dogs. It took him awhile, but he managed. Even the camp director thought Duke was going to jump like the other dogs. She was pretty nervous until I assured her

Duke would not jump. He knew what he was doing. He's smart like that.

People have asked us on several occasions if our dogs stay outside. *No way.* Our dogs with paralysis live in our home. We live in a one-level home with ramps and a fenced-in yard. We have sectioned off an area of our kitchen so all the dogs feel like they are part of our home and family. We needed to create this area because of their incontinence issues. We always keep plenty of cleaning supplies handy. We place clean towels and blankets down every morning and evening for them to sleep on. Dogs with disabilities still look forward to your coming home and going for a run or walk outside. As with any pet, it is all about routine. Eventually you get used to it. In the long run, I think caring for a dog with a disability is definitely worth it. You get *so much* out of the experience, and the memories you make last a lifetime.

What to Expect When
Living with a Blind Dog

Diane Francis and Steve Behnke,
Caretakers of Two Blind Dogs

Caring for a blind dog is a very challenging experience, but it is also extremely rewarding. The bottom line is you need to learn how to communicate with your dog in a way that he or she will understand and be able to communicate back with you. The catch is that visual communication is out of the question. Below are some techniques we use to interact with our blind dogs, Jaxx and Jesse, on a day-to-day basis:

1. Talking—I talk to Jaxx all the time about everything. Since his hearing is so good, this works extremely well. He knows where I am all the time, and by the tone of my voice he knows when it is safe or when it is not and that he needs to be cautious. Jaxx is very verbal and talks to me all the time too.
2. Consistency—I try to keep things exactly the way they are so he doesn't have to relearn where furniture is located or risk becoming confused and bumping into things around the

house. This helps him build on his strong sense of touch and his memory.

3. Assurance—Jaxx goes *everywhere* we go. We don't overprotect him, per se, but rather we encourage him to explore and develop his confidence in every situation. We take him on walks or we go up to the farm. Basically we go everywhere and do everything we would normally do with a dog that was not blind. We talk to him constantly so he knows where we are, and as he gains confidence he ventures farther up the path on his own. We try to always introduce him to new people and bring him into as many different situations as possible. He tends to adjust very quickly.

   I have the Invisible Fence installed at my home and at the farm. We trained Jaxx to be aware of it as one would train any dog—except rather than seeing the flags along the boundary lines, he *hears* them. He quickly learned his limitations and has never had any trouble. This is important for me, too, as I know he can go outside to do his business and play with the other dogs without constant supervision.

4. Another important aspect of living with and training a blind dog is tactile feel. In a sense, their paws have become their eyes. In my house there are three different types of floor covering: tile, hardwood, and carpet. Jesse knows all three and where they lead. If he is on the tile in the kitchen, he knows that the tile leads to the hardwood in the dining room, which leads to the carpet in the living room. He walks around just as if he can see. People are always amazed at his mobility.

5. Finally, sounds are most important. When I feed Jesse I always tell him that it's dinnertime. When I put his bowl down I make

sure to tap it loudly so that he knows where it is. Another feeding trick is to put a piece of plastic on the floor around the dish area. This goes back to the tactile feel of the floor. Once a dog realizes that the plastic leads to its food and water bowls, it will adapt very easily.

Good luck with training and becoming your blind dog's best friend. You're in for a wonderful experience!

Additional Resources

BONES Pet Rescue
Better Options for Neglected Strays
P.O. Box 1009
Covelo, CA 95428
707-983-6422
http://www.covelo.net/animal_rescue/bones.shtml

Bright Haven—A Nonprofit Holistic Animal Retreat
P.O. Box 1743
Sebastopol, CA 95473-1743
707-578-4800
http://www.brighthaven.org

Collie Rescue of Southeastern Pennsylvania
P.O. Box 493
Ambler, Pa 19002
215-793-9298
http://www.collierescueofsepa.org

Deaf Dog Education Action Fund
http://www.deafdogs.org

Dewey's Wheelchairs For Dogs
P.O. Box 1439
Prineville, OR 97754
877-312-2123
http://www.wheelchairsfordogs.com

Glen Highland Farm
217 Pegg Road
Morris, NY 13080
607-263-5415
http://www.glenhighlandfarm.com

Handicapped Pets
10 Northern Blvd, #7
Amherst, NH 03031
603-673-8854
http://www.handicappedpets.com

Pets with Disabilities
1010 Theater Drive
Prince Frederick, MD 20678
410-257-3141
http://www.petswithdisabilities.org

Rolling Dog Ranch Animal Sanctuary
400 Rolling Dog Ranch Lane
Ovando, MT 59854
406-793-6000
http://www.rollingdogranch.com

Spring Farm CARES
3364 State Rt. 12
Clinton, NY 13323
315-737-9339
http://www.springfarmcares.org

St. Francis Society Animal Rescue
P.O. Box 261614
Tampa, FL 33685-1614
813-961-5340
http://www.luvamutt.org

http://www.blinddogs.com
http://www.blinddogs.net
http://www.deafdogs.com